ADVANCE PRAISE

"This remarkable book faces and answers the challenge facing leaders worldwide today; namely, how to balance left brain linear thinking with the extraordinary capacity of the right brain to see the whole picture, and more. The skills of deep listening, empathy, inclusivity and compassion are now recognized and used by those making the wisest decisions in politics, the military, economics, law and justice, as well as in business. These are the skills required if humanity is to survive, and this book tells you how to access them."

DR SCILLA ELWORTHY

Three times nominated for the Nobel Peace Prize, founder of the Oxford Research Group, Peace Direct and the Business Plan for Peace

"Nicholas's book *Leader as Healer* gets to the heart of one of the major challenges facing leaders today. In the book, he skilfully outlines the path of a major element of becoming a 21st-century leader. I have no doubt many leaders will be transformed by this book, and that its impact will be felt by the colleagues, employees, customers, suppliers and society that they serve too."

ANDREW WHITE

Senior Fellow in Management Practice (Leadership), University of Oxford Said Business School

"Nicholas' insights, passion and unique ability to (re)connect leaders and their teams with their own humanity sets him apart as the most impactful leadership development coach I know and have personally benefited from. In a post COVID-19 world, the corporate world needs a new vision for leaders and leadership. This book delivers just that."

RUSSELL SHELDON

Chief Operations and Technology Officer, TMF Group

"If ever there was fulfilment upon the phrase 'leadership for our time,' this is it. Reading *Leader as Healer*, I immediately discovered a gift, an automatic deep resonance emerged in what is needed and desired by me. I am a fast paced, on the go, chronically responsible and over committed CEO, father, coach, husband, grandfather and friend, and I discovered a path to return home and be the best version of myself and a leader that heals. Nicholas is a master coach and now we can all engage and learn from him. It is a must read for any leader who wants to do and be better, produce greater results that feed and nurture, and produce a world where we all thrive. Thank you, Nicholas."

WILLIAM (BILL) ADAMS

CEO and co-founder, Leadership Circle

"In a world of uncertainties and suffering, *Leader as Healer* is a gift of wisdom, an insightful book for executives everywhere that catalyzes the connection between human beings and self-knowledge as the genesis of resilience, success and breakthrough."

RUBEN M FERNANDES

CEO Base Metals, Anglo American Plc

"It is difficult to overemphasize the importance of Nicholas Janni's book. Beautifully written and lucid, it addresses a fundamental fracture in the realm of business and political leadership. It's a vital resource in the realm of education, too. I will be quoting from this profound book with student groups all over the world because it speaks of a vital healing. If we are serious about providing young people with the best possible education, the beauty of academic reasoning alone will never be enough. This is a vast conversation, and this book tackles its key themes with both courage and clarity. I hope it will be another step to a time in which the inner journey Nicholas Janni describes has become central to the curriculum, alongside language development and mathematics."

BEN WALDEN

Director of the Contender Charlie company
– serving leadership development in education

"This is the sort of book the world needs right now, as volatility demands more than most are able to offer in our present state. It's provocative, compelling, and deeply practical. If you're a leader, you must read this book – and get ready to be transformed into a more generative state of being."

SAM ISAACSON

Author of *How to Thrive as a Coach in a Digital World*,
founder of Coachtech

"In this book, Nicholas offers practical tools that will inspire leaders to tap into their highest potential. Only in front of authentic, vulnerable and present leaders can people truly show up, express themselves and share their full value. This is a must-read book for any leader, regardless of their rank."

AMIR GLOGAU
Founder and Managing Partner, Citrine Capital Partners,
founder and CEO, Guidely

"I've been working with Nicholas both personally and professionally since 2014, and this book beautifully summarizes his views on what it takes to become a truly impactful leader. If we wish to be better leaders, we must become better human beings – making a difference not just through our words, but fundamentally through our presence, including deep sensitivity to those we lead and interact with. If you are a leader in any capacity, his ideas and practices will serve as a guidepost to leaning into your highest potential, into your next 'best self,' into becoming a *Leader as Healer.*"

DAVID GRAFFY
Former President, ProLift Industrial Equipment,
Class Leader, Stagen Leadership Academy

"Nicholas' expertise and wisdom serve as an invaluable compass in everyone's life journey to become a better version of who we are, and how we can reconnect with ourselves and others in a more meaningful way, as a person and as a leader. His guidance is practical, direct and more relevant than ever."

GEORGIOS LAMPAS
CFO, Osem Nestle, Israel

"Nicholas Janni has developed an approach to leadership development which is refreshing, challenging and optimistic. He offers ways of accessing all the personal resources at our disposal, unlocking perspectives and energy we may never have known we had or could use in our professional lives. For some this may feel unfamiliar, even uncomfortable – take a leap of faith and you will be rewarded."

ALICE PERKINS
CB Former HRD for the UK civil service with wide-ranging UK Board experience in the private and not-for-profit sectors, and business coach

"Nicholas truly understands the role of modern leadership and captures its very essence in *Leader as Healer.* I know from our work with him that his ability to connect with people and utilize methods that challenge leaders to deepen their understanding of themselves is remarkable."

AARON PUNA
Executive Vice President & Chief Technology Officer, Newmont Corporation

"Nicholas Janni shows in this book that he has the unique and precious ability to translate the insights and practices of ancient spiritual traditions into today's world and make them accessible for leaders from across different cultures, seniorities and functions. The impact of his work is profound and transformational."

ALBRECHT ENDERS
Professor of Strategy and Innovation, IMD Business School

"*Leader as Healer* is the answer to our modern-day crises. With so much complexity and unpredictability in our world, our leaders need new paradigms, mindsets, and tools. The answer is clear: we must develop our multiple levels of intelligence – our physical, emotional, and intellectual selves – to grow into the type of leader that can steward our organizations, communities, and planet towards positive change."

ALLISON TSAO

Founder and OD Consultant, Humans Who Lead

"Change is urgent in our fragmented world. *Leader as Healer* is essential reading for all those who seek to bring restoration and harmony within their lives and those they serve. Nicholas Janni teaches us that becoming whole, returning home to ourselves is the core place from which we are empowered to become extraordinary leaders. By offering the very best of ourselves, we present an unconditional gift to those we lead, rewarding and nurturing to both the leader and the led. We can look forwards to experiencing the significant contribution *Leader as Healer* is set to make towards a future in which well-being, innovation and success are naturally interwoven."

SALLY DUNSMORE

Festival Director, FT Weekend Oxford Literary Festival

"This book is critical for our times. Morale and employee engagement are at historic lows. If the leader is out of balance, their families and employees feel the impact. When the leader engages with the work Nicholas outlines, they positively impact their employees and help them create healthier teams and healthier families. And then we have energized communities and thriving organizations which, in turn, produce a healthier world."

MARK TAYLOR

Master Chair for Vistage International,
the world's largest executive coaching organization

"Nicholas Janni's book fills an enormous void among the approximately 60,000 books being sold on Amazon, which have the word 'leader' in the title. This book should be considered required reading for anyone in senior leadership of any kind."

EUGENE A WOODS

President and CEO, Atrium Health

"Nicholas Janni is a pioneer in transformational leadership and beautifully captures the zeitgeist in business. Presented as a modern-day path for a leader or a roadmap for organizational culture, he focuses on the importance of emotions, embodiment, relational attunement, higher purpose, mindfulness and service to life. Written from the heart of a seeker, the sensibility of a theatre director, the expertise of a top team coach and the vision of an activist, *Leader as Healer* is a primer for leading in the century ahead."

AMY ELIZABETH FOX

Chief Executive Officer, Mobius Executive Leadership

LEADER AS HEALER

A NEW PARADIGM FOR 21ST-CENTURY LEADERSHIP

NICHOLAS JANNI

JAICO PUBLISHING HOUSE

Ahmedabad Bangalore Chennai
Delhi Hyderabad Kolkata Mumbai

Published by Jaico Publishing House
A-2 Jash Chambers, 7-A Sir Phirozshah Mehta Road
Fort, Mumbai - 400 001
jaicopub@jaicobooks.com
www.jaicobooks.com

Published in arrangement with
LID Business Media Limited
LABS House, 15-19 Bloomsbury Way
London, WC1A 2TH, UK

To be sold only in India, Bangladesh, Bhutan,
Pakistan, Nepal, Sri Lanka and the Maldives.

LEADER AS HEALER
ISBN 978-93-49358-07-2

First Jaico Impression: 2025

Cover and page design: Caroline Li

Printed by
Trinity Academy For Corporate Training Limited, Mumbai

LEADER AS HEALER

CONTENTS

ACKNOWLEDGEMENTS

Julie Jordan Avritt, the sensitivity and brilliance of your editing work played an essential part in completing the final manuscript.

All at LID Publishing for your belief in the book: Alec Egan, Martin Liu, Aiyana Curtis, and Caroline Li for the artwork.

Special thanks to:

William Ayot and Scilla Elworthy, the length and depth of our friendships and collaborations, and the gifts, courage and wisdom you each bring to the world has enriched my life immeasurably.

Michael Watkins, your support and our personal and professional relationships over all these years mean the world to me.

Gene Woods, for all that you are, for all that we have shared and for all that is to come.

Andrew White, such a joy to witness your evolution and the richness of our dialogues.

Michelle McMurry-Heath, our work together has been profoundly humbling and inspiring.

Close friendships in which we can share both the greatest inspirations and the darkest moments are a core part of what make my life worthwhile. My deep thanks to Joey Walters, Malcolm Stern, Katherine Menton, Shoshana Heller, Ben Walden, Sola Akingbola, Antonia Guarini, Giuseppe Goffredo, Amir Glogau, David Graffy and Gary Joplin.

Gratitude to all the members of the ongoing groups I ran in UK, US and Israel, who engaged personal, intergenerational and collective trauma work with such commitment. And particular thanks to Christine Gerike and Robert Buxbaum for our mutual learning journey with the New York group.

My work with leaders began over 25 years ago and led to the co-creation of Oliver Mythodrama. Thanks to Richard Olivier and all at OMA for the adventure and collaborations.

And Yael Shazar, for your tireless efforts to bring the work to Israel.

Kahu Abraham Kawai'i and Thomas Hubl, two spiritual masters, with whom the long periods of shattering initiatory study brought quantum learning and evolution. And Master Mingtong Gu for the glorious gift of Qigong in my daily life.

I bow with awe to my children Leila and Gabriel and stepdaughter Gabriella, as I witness the way each of you, so different, is becoming a mature, powerful, sensitive person, having such impact in the world.

And my wife Hadassa, without whom none of this would have been possible. Your brilliance, creativity, beauty, empathy and fierceness shine ever more strongly. The many dimensions of our intimacy are more than I could have ever imagined or hoped for.

FOREWORD
BY EUGENE A WOODS

From a worldwide pandemic to a depression-era economy, to the racial strife sparked by the killing of George Floyd to the cavernous divisions and discord in our global politics, to being on the precipice of climate catastrophe — the years 2020–22 have felt like our entire societal structures were crumbling beneath our very feet. The truth is, old and outmoded social forms have been deconstructing for some time; it's just that the fault lines have now been fully exposed.

So, where do we go from here? How do we 'fix' things? What is required of us as individuals and as leaders? In his book, *Leading from the Emerging Future: From Ego-System to Eco-System Economies*, C Otto Scharmer of MIT's Sloan School of Management concludes: "This is the moment when what we need most is enough people with the skill, heart, and wisdom to help us pull ourselves back from the edge of breakdown and onto a different path."[1] Yes, but how does one develop the "skill, heart, and wisdom" to address the intractable and deeply rooted systematic challenges that confront us?

My good friend and coach Nicholas Janni has developed this guidebook, which answers that very question and fills the enormous void among the approximately 60,000 books being sold on Amazon that have the word 'leader' in the title. Nicholas takes us on an experiential journey that starts with coming home to our bodies, embracing our emotions, expanding our bandwidth and mental capacity, aligning with our deepest purpose, liberating our creativity and returning home to silence.

I was first introduced to Nicholas several years ago through a mutual friend, Michael Watkins, the international bestselling author of *The First 90 Days*. Our meeting occurred shortly after I'd taken the helm as CEO of a $10 billion healthcare system, with nearly 70,000 employees and 50 hospitals. When I met Nicholas, not only was I starting a new job, in a new city – and chairing the American Hospital Association board during a tumultuous period in the healthcare field – but I was also in the middle of a divorce, living unsettled among boxes in a yet-to-be renovated home, all the while attempting to support my son's difficult emotional transition to a new school.

I have always been able to carry a heavy load on my shoulders, but the metre was starting to hit the red zone and I needed someone to help me process it all. Having worked with many coaches in the past, what I came to appreciate about Nicholas was that he had a completely different orientation and approach. More than anything, he helped ground me in my true purpose: that *healing* is my fundamental calling as a leader. Thereafter, my lens on work and the world completely changed.

I have devoted my life's work to leading nationally prominent health care systems – the places people come to during their most vulnerable moments in search of healing. They come for physical healing, of course. But broken bodies often come with broken spirits, which are every bit as much in need of healing. And what I realized in my sessions with Nicholas is that, too often, we see other humans in bits and pieces, rather than as integrated wholes. Why? Because we experience our own inner lives in a very fragmented manner.

To truly lead and connect, healing must begin with us.

With the deftness of an expert guide who has long travelled his own journey of self-discovery, Nicholas's direction is clear, precise and comes from a non-judgemental heart. During dark days, he held a navigational light, illuminating my way so that I could begin to unfreeze and integrate parts of myself – both the personal and the ancestral – which had become like 'frozen blocks of energy.'

To be clear, the journey to one's healing is never complete. But, the work so far has already significantly expanded my bandwidth and effectiveness as a leader, which includes my ability to foster a healing environment for others so that they can expand theirs.

This book should be considered required reading for anyone in senior leadership, because we are at a moment in the world in which the need for leaders who can bring about true societal healing has never been more consequential to the survivability of our businesses or social and political institutions – or to us as a species. Beyond that, we all yearn for true connection, and this book, or rather, this dialogue, addresses that, as well. May it be for you a dialogue of discovery around what it means to bring integrated wholeness to leadership, with the service of healing as the first order of priority.

Above all, Nicholas has written an essential guide to help you to discover what it means to be a *Leader as Healer.*

EUGENE A WOODS

President and Chief Executive Officer, Atrium Health

INTRODUCTION

FROM LEADER AS EXECUTOR TO LEADER AS HEALER

This is a book about the highest levels of presence and peak performance leadership, and the cultures that ensue from them, in which wellbeing, results and contribution to the world are naturally interwoven.

It is, above all, a call to break from the chronically imbalanced ways of thinking and functioning that have become the norm in so many corporate cultures, where 'doing' eclipses 'being,' and hyper-rational, analytical thinking relegates feeling, sensing, intuiting and the transpersonal to the outer fringes of life.

I believe that the failure to correct this imbalance is severely detrimental not only to individual and organizational performance, but to our capacity for creating healthy, thriving futures.

In the book, I outline a theoretical and practical path to a new paradigm of leadership. It is a path of *restoration* through which we reintegrate previously exiled aspects of our nature: physical, emotional and transpersonal. On this pathway, the brilliance and sophistication of the thinking self takes its rightful place alongside the sensing and feeling selves, together creating a much larger, more holistic intelligence.

To face the scope and threats of 21st-century challenges, today's leaders must possess potent powers for logic, reason, discernment and strategic forecasting. Yet, they must also be empathic and, therefore, embodied; grounded and, therefore, intuitive. They must be skilled in mindfulness and deep listening; present and receptive to higher levels of insight and innovation; able to inspire authentic engagement and collaboration; and possess a clear and wholehearted sense of service, mission and purpose.

I call this leader the *Leader as Healer.*

This is a path of restoration,
through which we reintegrate
previously exiled aspects
of our nature: physical,
emotional and transpersonal.

No one can doubt the incredible impact of the last few years on our organizational environments. From radically shifting markets, the impact of a global climate emergency to the COVID-19 pandemic, accelerating disruption, instability and unpredictability have created a leadership litmus test. Some leaders have stepped up magnificently, mobilizing their companies or nations to respond effectively to these and other challenges while at the same time projecting compassion and offering needed reassurance. Their people trust them.

Many leaders, however, attempt to meet these unprecedented challenges from the context of an old and dying model of governance. As a result, they are left unable or unwilling to act decisively on behalf of their stakeholders and constituents. We should not be surprised – they work according to the models and mindsets they have been taught from an early age, and which our cultures have normalized. All too frequently, these leaders also operate out of overt or covert self-interest, prioritizing and protecting their own positions. They offer no security, foundation of resilience or credibility from which to weather the psychological and economic turbulence. The actions of such leaders induce fractures, mistrust and dysfunction among their people.

In these vastly divergent responses, I see two models of leadership at play: the Leader as Executor and the Leader as Healer.

In recent decades, as the world has driven for growth and efficiency above all else, the Leader as Executor became the dominant global business model, the prevailing standard that sees 'great' leaders as drivers of action and agents of discipline. Their relationships are transactional, and their goals are primarily instrumental: maximize profit and shareholder returns. The power of Executors rests in a metaphorical sword to be wielded on the perpetual battlefield of business competition. And it is a war of attrition.

Executors operate from a narrow bandwidth, characterized by the primacy of the rational, strategic mind. They are generally disconnected from their emotional and physical selves, which creates an absence of deep listening and receptivity. Executors function almost constantly in a 'doing' modality with little or no access to 'being.'

But all models must evolve to meet changing circumstances.

The global COVID-19 crisis has exposed executor-oriented leadership for what it now is: inadequate to meet the huge systemic challenges facing us in 'the new abnormal.' It is inadequate because the rational, linear mind always seeks to reduce everything into knowable, predictable, replicable terms. Yet, the increasing complexity of our times cannot and will not yield to such an approach. To thrive, not merely survive amidst heightened disruption requires all new strategic competencies, heightened levels of innovative thinking and advanced capacities for receptivity and openness.

That execution-oriented leadership is still regarded as the gold standard, the model by which all others must operate, is testament to how entrenched we have become in a paradigm that no longer serves us. Blind adherence to this outmoded style creates leaders who are no longer fit for purpose and a modality of function that poses a threat to the long-term health of our societies.

I find in my work that most executives instinctively know when they are leading in an unbalanced and unsustainable way. They know it because of the stress and frustration it induces. They know it because of the lack of meaning and connection and, sometimes, even despair they experience. Yet, in the field of business education, there is remarkably little emphasis or instruction on the inner development of the leader, or the emotional, ethical and spiritual maturity that is required of them. People are thrust into senior positions of responsibility with a lack of preparation that, in many other fields, would be unthinkable.

Even before the pandemic, many chief executives and senior leaders were speaking about the new capacities they realized they needed to develop in increasingly unpredictable environments. Chief amongst these: being comfortable with uncertainty, and able to embrace paradox, doubt and ambiguity without rushing to an ineffective fix. They revealed a growing need to meet and adapt to complexity with much more than the linear, formulaic strategies of the past. Since the pandemic, instability has grown exponentially. One of my CEO clients recently said to me: "I am understanding more and more that I simply cannot lead, cannot formulate strategy, in any of the ways I did before. I am in a completely new land."

Individually and collectively, we find ourselves more than ever engulfed in a volatility, uncertainty, complexity and ambiguity (VUCA) environment. Recently, a new acronym entered the corporate lexicon: Brittle, Anxious, Non-linear and Incomprehensible (BANI). The growing scale of the systemic challenges before us is far beyond anything we have faced before. To meet the moment, we need new frameworks of understanding and higher capacities with which to lead. Today's leaders must be able to embrace complexity, grapple with ambiguity, and express authentic empathy. They must learn to access the wisdom and emotional skill required to steer the ship in a rapidly changing world. They must be people who seek opportunities for genuine inner development, for themselves and those they lead. They must be able and willing to create cultures of real engagement in which people give the best of themselves, and experience the deep satisfaction that comes with seeking to contribute more than to take.

AN EMERGING MODEL – LEADER AS HEALER

In the context of leadership, *healing* does not refer to the physical. Rather, it is:

- The *restoration of unity*, bringing those parts of us and the systems within which we work that are fragmented and/or exiled back into a coherent whole
- The *rebalancing* of our thinking, emotional and physical selves
- The *transformation* of stagnant energy, leading to greater vitality, enhanced connection, and higher intelligence and wisdom
- The *awakening* of transpersonal levels of consciousness
- And a precise *excision* of that which is toxic, unhealthy and dangerous to the whole

Healers are leaders who have highly developed rational minds and have likewise invested in their emotional and psychological development. They are leaders who transmit embodied presence. They have explored and sufficiently reintegrated wounded parts of themselves and developed higher levels of consciousness and innovative capacity, abilities described by all cultures for thousands of years. As a result, these leaders bring to the table their cognitive, emotional and embodied physical selves; no part of the whole is excluded.

The Leader as Healer sees the world, its problems and potential solutions in very different ways than the Leader as Executor. The Healer can analyse and strategize every bit as well as the Executor, but knows what it means to connect with themself and others, to integrate being and doing, proactivity and receptivity, rationality and intuition.

The Healer both understands and embodies the essence of coherent presence: *I'm here, and I'm available.* They recognize the power of fostering connection and know, for instance, that just one minute of quality attention paid to a colleague or employee is priceless. Where the Executor builds cultures of absence on a foundation of disconnection, the Healer creates cultures of presence on a foundation of interconnection.

Critically, the Healer utilizes power very differently than the Executor. In place of the sword, a Healer chooses the scalpel. He or she understands that feeling and empathy are essential, but not always sufficient. True leadership sometimes requires that one decisively excise moral and spiritual tumours from the bodies of organizations or nations. And, like all good surgeons, Healers seek to preserve any and all healthy tissue, to the greatest extent possible.

This emergent model of leadership unlocks parts of ourselves that have long been pushed aside, and even derided, in order to expand our operating bandwidth. By bringing higher levels of consciousness to our work, we find we can access much more nuanced information, much subtler signals. We can unlock new reserves of energy and inspiration, elevating our efforts and those of our teams to higher levels of efficiency, innovation and impact.

This style of leadership is a journey that demands transformational inner work and uncovers new reserves of wisdom and empathy. It is a path that marries the sophistication of rationality and the brilliance of science to the profound understandings of timeless wisdom and cutting-edge body-mind psychology, better preparing us to meet the times in which we live.

This fresh and necessarily radical vision offers an entirely new perspective on leadership. As we face 'the new abnormal,' the prior model is no longer enough. Simply put, execution-style leadership doesn't cut it. As Albert Einstein advised, we cannot solve our problems with the same thinking we used to create them.

It is time for a new toolbox.

EXPANDING OUR BANDWIDTH

In the old paradigm, most leaders take in information, strategically analyse and assess, and then roll out a solution without recourse to our emotional, intuitive and physical selves. Indeed, many cultures, both societal and organizational, mistakenly conflate emotion with weakness and unpredictability. Emotion is regarded as wholly unproductive. We labour under the illusion that there is such a thing as a purely rational decision. Yet, in more than 40 years, I have not witnessed a single example of purely rational decision-making when the stakes are high.

Because, without exception, all the leaders I have met carry within themselves an assemblage of unattended hurts, scars and fears, originating in childhood and adolescence, and including intergenerational and systemic family patterns. This is an inevitable, natural part of our humanity. That these wounds remain unaddressed is unsurprising; there is rarely an opportunity to safely and responsibly process the pain of the past. But such injuries do not just disappear. To the contrary, they take up space in the present as frozen blocks of energy, controlling our drives, numbing our hearts and limiting our vitality, vision and relational capacities. As the great psychoanalyst Carl Jung said: "Until you make the unconscious conscious, it will direct your life and you will call it fate."

We are all familiar with the success of toxic CEOs who remain unchallenged and unrestrained due to the antiquated organizational norms and dysfunctional power structures that allow them to exist. Many of the highest-profile world leaders emerged from family backgrounds in which shame, hostility and even violence were the norm. For many of them, unhealed childhood adversity will lead to unregulated emotions, interpersonal difficulty, narcissistic tendencies[2] and even sociopathic personality structures,[3] all of which spell grave consequences for people and organizations.

The cultures in which toxic leaders hold the greatest power are those that uphold the outmoded belief that traits like empathy, vulnerability and connection equate to weakness. (After all, these characteristics have historically been associated with women.) Executors endorse these biases, while Healers dismantle them. The Leader as Healer understands that unless we acknowledge our grief, we cannot feel our joy; unless we embrace our fear, we cannot know true strength; unless we learn to embrace emotions unconditionally, we limit our access to higher levels of intelligence and insight. And that, until we remember what it is to live in an embodied state, our experience of the rich multi-dimensionality of life is enormously reduced.

In my experience with hundreds of clients, both one-on-one and in groups, I have found that when leaders feel safe enough to directly feel and articulate their emotions – in healthy and appropriate ways – entirely positive outcomes result. When we stop fighting or denying our anxieties and fears, for instance, we find that, once embraced, they ground us more deeply in the body, open our energy, and allow us to better relate to and connect with others. When a group of senior leaders feels secure enough to speak openly with one another about so-called 'difficult' emotions, breakthroughs of connectedness and understanding almost always follow. When we create space to attend to our fears, sadness and frustrations, our defensive strategies soften. We become more accepting, more compassionate, more embracing of ourselves and the world. And then, a portal to new ideas and solutions invariably opens.

A colleague of mine described a recent programme he ran with 15 chief executives. After a writing exercise that allows for deep expression, each person was invited to speak their written words to the group. He knew that at least three people in the room had lost friends or colleagues to COVID-19. One woman was too emotional to speak. My colleague knelt in front of her, facing the group. He asked her permission to speak her words and invited her to put her hand on his shoulder. As he spoke, the hearts in the room palpably melted. After he finished reading, there was a natural, vibrantly charged silence, after which a wave of new ideas and insights came flooding into the group.

This is how energy works. When all of the physical tension we use to suppress emotion is relaxed, our bodies deeply settle as that formerly blocked energy is freed. Now that it can flow, it naturally metabolizes into a resource for dynamic individual and group intelligence. When these emotional energies remain blocked, however, we operate on a narrower bandwidth, less able to feel or sense clearly, and therefore less able to be fully present for ourselves and others.

Sadly, and dangerously, the latter mode of operation is the norm in Western cultures, where mainstream education focuses almost exclusively on the rational mind and the practical achievements it can produce. In this paradigm, we prioritize the accumulation of knowledge at the expense of creativity, play or connection. We relegate nature to the role of an exterior problem, to be controlled and conquered. Our relationships become predominantly transactional; we talk to but rarely *feel* each other. We learn to hear without truly listening. We become consumed by task orientation: constant action, incessant doing. Our participation in life is compromized and we are prevented from enjoying a more direct experience of the world. This all leads to what I call a *culture of absence*, which is a state of separation and collective numbness.

It is a cruel irony that, while we live in a time of accelerating digital connectivity, we have never been more isolated and disconnected.

It is indeed a cruel irony that, while we live in a time of accelerating digital connectivity, we have never been more isolated. We see around us an epidemic of anxiety, depression and loneliness, particularly in the younger generation, and an increasingly fractured society coming undone by social conflict, political polarization, insatiable consumption, and potentially terminal planetary destruction. To avoid the painful truth, we bury ourselves in the excesses of materialism and so-called productivity. We miss out on true purpose, inspiration and relationship, through which we might experience the power of heartfelt human encounters and a more visceral sense of the landscapes and environments we inhabit.

It is time to awaken from this state of exile and disconnection. As we do so, an inner stillness settles in and grows, enabling us to perceive ourselves and our lives in gradually more multi-layered, multi-faceted ways. As this unfolds, our habitual drives and prior distractions hold less influence. Qualities of embodied connectedness and presence become the dominant guiding principles of our lives and our work.

A leader who knows how to guide others into such fertile territory invariably finds that meetings become more enhanced, energized and often inspired, and that an altogether higher order of collective intelligence unfolds. It is an intelligence that is more urgently needed than ever.

Humanity is at a critical juncture. We must change or face dire, even existential, consequences. Organizations stuck in old-paradigm leadership may well face extinction. An executive at Switzerland's IMD business school recently approached me during a break to say: "I work for a traditional, 80-year-old Swiss firm that has always held the top position in our field. We have a new competitor who we predict will take that position within five years. Our old-style board cannot understand how this is happening. I see clearly now: they are doing what we are learning in this programme. That's why they have so much energy, connection and innovation."

Do we continue to endorse leaders who are detached and emotionally unavailable, who are incapable of truly relating or listening, and who remain restricted to a narrow bandwidth of linear thinking? Or do we seek and develop leaders who are fully engaged, deeply attuned and receptive? Leaders who are self-aware, emotionally warm, and devoted to lives of meaningful contribution. Leaders willing to hold open a window to new ideas.

In his book, *The Master and his Emissary*, the psychiatrist and Oxford University All Souls scholar Iain McGilchrist goes so far as to say that, in his view, the current imbalance between left- and right-brain thinking – specifically, the dominance of the former – poses the single biggest threat to the survival of our civilization.[4] Our operating model of indefatigable consumption and endless economic growth is leading us to the cliff's edge. In the face of ever-increasing complexity, unpredictability and change, the need for individuals, organizations and societies to access higher evolutionary potentials is more important, and more urgent, than ever.

A NEW PATH

This book is a call for a new type of leadership, one based on the integration of all the parts of who we are, and for the higher-performance teams and advanced organizational cultures that naturally follow. I believe that our willingness to engage in and occupy this integration is critical in determining how well we can navigate the challenges we face and to the type of future we will create.

The principles and practices offered in these pages are applicable to all types and levels of leadership: they are laid out through theory, examples and practical exercises designed to help leaders bring all of their faculties forwards. This then empowers leaders to build embodied, energized cultures of connectedness, founded on presence and receptivity to higher levels of insight and innovation. This approach has been tried and tested by hundreds of leaders, with clear, transformational results.

The pages ahead will take you through the principles and the application of becoming a Leader as Healer. They are meant to be used and revisited as much and as often as you need. Make notes, take time to ingest the ideas and let them inspire you towards new ways of leading, and thereby serving, our world.

It begins with a foundational principle and then addresses the inner work needed in five interdependent aspects:

- Foundation – Doing and Being
- Embracing Emotions
- The Power of Embodiment
- Living a Life of Purpose
- The Practice of Mindfulness and Meditation
- The Call

Throughout the book you will also:

- Learn many simple, practical exercises and tools for becoming a Leader as Healer
- Discover how this eminently practical and genuinely transformational approach has been embraced by other leaders

Some years ago, I had the privilege of an audience with a famous Rabbi in Israel. Knowing of my work with leaders, he concluded our meeting by declaring that there was one essential message he wished to convey. He said that one of the deepest callings of the Abrahamic faith is to 'be a blessing,' and that he wished for all leaders to remember that call.

This book may well challenge the way you have been brought up, how you work and the reality in which you live. But there is nothing more inspiring – and nothing more urgently needed – than leaders who include the very best of rational thinking while operating from a deeper level of wisdom, connectedness and intelligence.

They are the ones who walk in the world as a blessing.

Our future is at stake.

The time is now.

CHAPTER 1

FOUNDATION: BEING AND DOING

There are two fundamental modes from which we all operate: *Being* and *Doing*. Being arises from our receptive, emotional and sensing self, while doing describes action directed from the rational, analytical, strategic mind. These two distinct modes have their own unique capacities and competencies, yet are deeply complementary. In an ideal world, we would utilize being and doing in tandem, and each mode would have equal influence on our perceptual and behavioural processes.

Being and doing speak to the different halves of the human brain. The notion that the two cerebral hemispheres execute entirely different and unrelated functions – the left for logic and the right for creativity – is now recognized as an over-simplification. Researchers have determined that, while each has unique characteristics, the hemispheres work together to efficiently and effectively complete tasks. The left hemisphere supports clear focus and rational analysis, while the right allows for broader, reflective sensory connection and intuitive thinking.

In virtually all the leaders and organizations with whom I have worked, doing dominates being. Despite our best efforts, we frequently get caught in cycles of action and execution, ignoring or diminishing the importance of 'beingness.' When did you last sit in silence for five minutes before a Zoom call in order to feel more embodied, composed and available? When was the last time you chaired a meeting and paused to ask how everyone was feeling? If you *have* done this, how many colleagues simply rattled through all of the problems they were working on?

Your answers to these questions likely reveal the common imbalance: the extent to which we vastly prioritize doing over being. Collectively, we are so focused on solving problems – ticking tasks off our to-do lists and moving on to the next thing – that our strategic minds have taken over. Hyper-focus on doing has detached us from our emotional and sensing selves, and therefore limited by at least half the intelligence and internal resources we bring to our work. The left brain has effectively subjugated the right.

This constricts our access to a wider field of information and inhibits our capacity to clearly sense and effectively respond to ourselves, one another and the work of our organizations in these times of ever-growing complexity and turbulence. By utilizing only one part of our processing power, it is as if we navigate the world with one hand tied behind our backs, in what I call a 'narrow bandwidth.' We think, think, think, and all too rarely feel, sense or intuit.

As MIT academics Otto Scharmer and Katrin Kaufer write in *Leading from the Emerging Future*: "Learning to tolerate the 'don't know mind,' or just being still, holding the whole in awareness, not having to know anything. This is the true inner work of redirection – and almost the opposite of the conditioning of most managers. The chronic shortcoming of many planned change efforts is blind adherence to 'the plan,' which reproduces the same unconscious mindsets. Operating from larger intention brings into play forces one could never tap from just trying to impose our will on a situation."[5]

Yet, even if, as the authors say, this is the opposite of our conditioning, we all have moments where we experience ourselves and the world in a more open way. Remember how, after a really great massage, your shoulders seem to drop two inches. You instantly feel looser, more relaxed. Only then do you realize that you had been walking around with your shoulders up by your ears, taut and tense. Yet, this state had seemed unquestionably normal, especially when everyone else is walking around this way too!

Or think of a time you participated in a great yoga or exercise class. Afterwards, maybe you stepped outside and, at least for a short time, reality felt different – more vivid and electric. You felt more alive, more connected to yourself and everything around you. You may even have wondered why this feeling is the exception, why the 'normal' reality in which you participate is actually such a compromised version of life.

In developmental terms, these are crucial moments of *subject-object* shift.[6] Tense shoulders, dulled perceptions and the dominance of doing over being are so much a part of the background that we have little perspective on them. These states are all just a part of life, a part of us (the subject). In key moments, however, we come to recognize these states as *objects* in awareness, meaning that we can observe them. We can witness their distinctness and reflect on their implications. In terms of development, subject-object transcendence is a crucial, game-changing step. I see its importance again and again in my one-on-one work with clients and with groups: once a new experience of connection to self and other occurs, our perspective irrevocably changes. A new horizon opens and, even though sustained practice is often required to dismantle old habits of 'absence,' a whole new pathway is made available.

This book is about choosing to walk down that pathway.

RELOCATION OF THE SELF

As we learn to practice mindfulness and skilfully combine feeling and sensing with logic and reason, we begin to shift our identity from the periphery of ourselves and operate from a deeper well, a deeper central axis. We shift and broaden the locus of our awareness so that it becomes more inclusive, more whole. We relocate from the identity of 'I as thinker' to 'I as Presence who thinks, feels and senses.'

This is the game-changer.

We can think of being and doing as two forms of movement or circles: when rational thinking governs, we tend to proceed along a forward trajectory. As we gain momentum in this direction, we move upwards and out of ourselves – literally away from contact with our bodies – towards a more peripheral, disembodied location, largely at or near the level of the head. This is a 'forward circle'.

We mistakenly take this as the normal way of relating to the world while, in fact, it is the basis of a narrow bandwidth. But, as we begin to bring being to the fore, we sense ourselves moving back and 'down,' as if dropping back into our bodies, and everything changes. We feel more embodied, more rooted in the self. This is a 'backward circle', and the foundation of a much broader bandwidth. With this subtle yet crucial relocation, we think more clearly, while also being able to access more and more of our innate resources and meet the world much more alert and awake. (We will continue to explore the power of this process in subsequent chapters.)

When in get-the-job-done mode, we quickly and automatically take in what others say, analyse their words and react, all without much conscious feeling or sensing. We have little interior space or real receptivity. But true listening is all about *receiving* the other, which requires being open and available to *hear* what they say, to *sense* into their perspective, to *feel* their interior emotional landscape and *allow* their words and sentiments to land in us. When we listen in this way, our actions – our doing – come from a far more responsive and informed place.

The powerful thing about this kind of listening is that it does not take more time than rote listening. On the contrary, deeper listening actually saves time because our responses are more accurate and attuned. Moreover, it enriches our connections and allows us to think together and collaborate in our actions with greater clarity, discernment and innovation.

PRACTICE – FROM THE FORWARD CIRCLE TO THE BACKWARD CIRCLE

Many of my clients find the embodiment of this metaphor a vivid and extremely effective resource.

Start by deliberately engendering a forward circle – feel yourself moving up and away from the lower part of your body, then forward and out towards the world. Notice how your breathing becomes shallower and you begin to lose your sense of sitting, of your legs and feet. Your bandwidth of perception becomes narrower.

Then, pause and take a few deep breaths.

Use the exhalation to begin to move back in and down. With each outbreath, feel the release of tension and settle in your chair. Feel your legs more, and your feet and their contact with the ground. Allow your eyes to soften.

Now you are experiencing life from the 'backward circle,' from a base of being. Notice how you may begin to feel more available to the world around you, more ready to listen. As you continue practicing, you may also find that your mind becomes clearer and more receptive.

> The more often you practice this each day — especially before and during any meeting you attend, whether as participant or leader — the more you will feel its transformative effect.
>
> The message is simple: when you notice yourself on the 'forward circle,' get off.

The practice of relocating to encompass the principle of being brings a deep sense of inner settling, a feeling of coming home. As this gradually becomes 'the new normal,' it seems obvious to us that this is how we are supposed to be, and that the subjugation of being by *doing* is not only costly in terms of our personal effectiveness, but a dangerous aberration in our collective decision-making.

Let's explore the modalities in more detail.

PEAK PERFORMANCE PRESENCE
LEADER AS HEALER

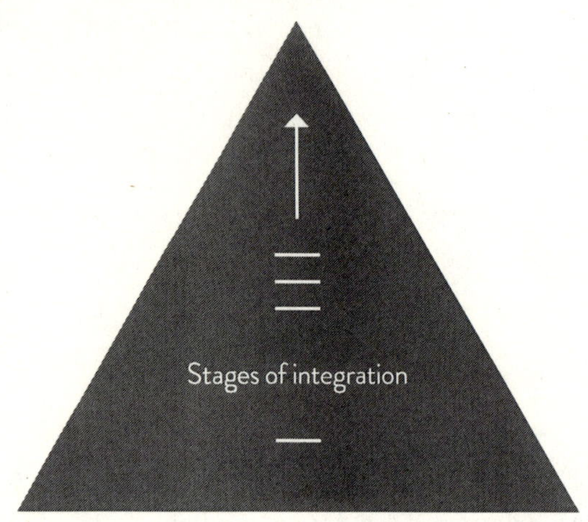

DOING	**BEING**
Left Brain	Right Brain
Proactive	Receptive/Reflective
Rational	Intuitive
Analytical	Empathic/Sensory
Form	Space
YANG	YIN

1) **LEFT BRAIN/RIGHT BRAIN.** The left and right cerebral hemispheres allow us to perceive reality in different ways: the left is detail-oriented, while the right is whole-oriented. The left allows rational analysis, focusing on distinct parts of a system with boundless sophistication. The right hemisphere allows a direct relationship with the physical body, and with external reality as represented by the senses, thus enabling a *felt* relationship with the world around us.

2) **PROACTIVE/RECEPTIVE, REFLECTIVE.** Being able to act effectively and efficiently in a proactive way is a crucial operational capacity, while the ability to sit back, absorb and reflect without seeking quick solutions provides an essential balance. Sometimes, we need to take a metaphorical (or literal) walk in the woods, or a walk around the lake. If proactivity is our overriding drive, we easily miss the subtler insights and solutions that arise from a deeper form of listening and reflection.

3) **RATIONAL/INTUITIVE.** Rationality is an incredible capacity, but when it operates at the expense of intuition we become blind to a fuller informational field, the richness and extent of which the rational mind cannot imagine. In his book, *The Metaphoric Mind: A Celebration of Consciousness*, Bob Samples tells us: "Albert Einstein called the intuitive or metaphoric mind a sacred gift. He added that the rational mind was a faithful servant. It is paradoxical that in the context of modern life we have begun to worship the servant and defile the divine."[7]

4) **ANALYTICAL/SENSORY, EMPATHIC.** The ability to analyse a system through its parts is a priceless tool, but equally precious is the capacity to feel and sense ourselves and our surroundings. Analysing without feeling and sensing other people and situations means we are using less than half of our processing capacity.

5) **FORM/SPACE.** The Jewish mystical tradition teaches that when we open the page of a book, there are black letters *and* a white page. In the 'doing' modality, we fixate solely on the black letters. With higher integration, we learn to perceive both the letters and the page, which greatly upgrades our operating system – we play on a much bigger game board. The white page is the ground of creativity, the inner field in which ideas 'come to us.' When we lose access to the white page, we condemn ourselves to a partial and incomplete perspective. (I explore these concepts further in Chapter 5.)

6) **YIN/YANG.** In the East, the two modalities of being and doing have long been recognized as yin and yang, complimentary halves that comprise the core principles at the heart of life. The ancient and well-known intertwined Tai chi symbol depicts the integration of both modalities, representing polarity as well as harmony and balance: the healthy functioning of body, heart, mind and spirit.

LEADERSHIP AS A HEALING ENDEAVOUR

The Leader as Healer repairs the disconnection between being and doing, dissolving fragmentation and the struggle of polarization by reuniting or integrating the two modalities. This occurs first within ourselves, and then in and with the people we lead. Through this process, we achieve deeper unity and coherence, both internally and externally. By bringing mind, body and heart into all we do, we access far more advanced responses to problems, challenges and opportunities. And we become able to access and operate from a much larger field of possibility.

A participant in a leadership programme once asked, "So, how much time should I spend being, and how much time should I spend doing?" We laughed together as it became immediately clear where the question was coming from!

By bridging the modalities, we reach optimum performance. All doing arises from the inner resource of being. Integration looks like the diagram below: a 'bowl' of being, out of which arises all doing – slow or fast, simple or complex. The strangled dichotomy of cognition versus emotion, or rationality versus intuition, disappears and the complimentary modalities come to operate in tandem and at the highest level.

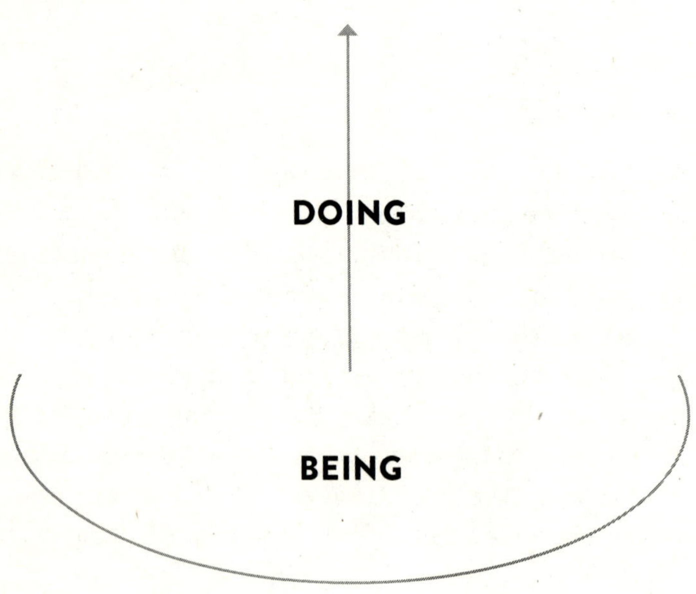

'Being' provides the balanced foundation from which we may respond rather than simply react. The Leader as Healer utilizes their left brain, or doing modality, to the full, while maximizing the functions of feeling and sensing. By relocating into beingness, the Leader as Healer is able to enfold rich emotional, intuitive and sensing capacities, and thereby amplify their processing power. Our doing is fast, slow, subtle, direct, gentle, fierce – *whatever it needs to be*, arising from our attunement to the person, environment or challenge we face.

Leaders as Healers cultivate unity between action and reflection, proactivity and receptivity, and analytical and intuitive competencies. They respond (rather than react) to themselves and others from an integrated foundation: *I am here, and I am available*. It is this inner coherence that creates a vital and profound leadership presence and transmits it into the environment.

QUESTIONS FOR REFLECTION:

- How do the modalities of Doing and Being operate in your life and in your leadership?
- When and how do you experience these modalities in integration — the bowl of Being, out of which all Doing arises?
- What are the gateways that allow you to touch an inner sense of Being (e.g., activities, places, people, art forms)? Might you need to give them a higher priority?

NEUROSCIENTIFIC AND ACADEMIC PERSPECTIVES

As we see with the concept of yin and yang, the notion that we all express two complementary polarities has been a part of many ancient wisdom traditions. In the modern world, researchers in neuroscience and other fields have begun to look closely at the effects that meditation and mindfulness have on the brain. They have found, for example, that these practices promote focus and attention and yield many other benefits, such as a reduction in anxiety and depression.[8]

In fact, meditation and mindfulness measurably alter brain wave frequency, allowing practitioners to move from beta waves – those seen in ordinary waking consciousness, for the completion of routine tasks – towards deeper alpha, theta and delta wave states. The latter not only enhance focused relaxation and flow states, but also learning, memory and intuition, as well as regeneration and repair.[9]

Dr Iain McGilchrist has widely explored the left and right hemispheres of the brain. While both are needed for every function, he says, each brings something unique to the task. He describes the left hemisphere as the seat of focused, narrow attention, while the right allows for broader and more sustained focus, and supports vigilance and alertness.[10] In his landmark book, *The Master and His Emissary: The Divided Brain and the Making of the Western World*, McGilchrist offers fascinating observations. "The relationship between the two hemispheres does not appear to be symmetrical," he writes, "in that the left hemisphere is ultimately dependent on, one might almost say parasitic on, the right, though it seems to have no awareness of this fact."[11]

Synthesizing many years of research, McGilchrist concludes that because the right hemisphere has a direct relationship with the physical body and the external world around us, it is a mediator for all we do. The right brain senses the wider world and passes information to the left brain for analysis. The left brain then returns its analysis so that, with wider, more holistic perception, we can determine how best to respond.

McGilchrist likens the left-brain takeover to an old tale of a wise king who, as tradition demanded, took an annual walk round his entire kingdom. As the kingdom grew, the king could no longer make the whole walk, so he enlisted and trained an emissary to assist him: to observe, process and report back. The emissary grew over-confident, however, and decided to go it alone, usurping his ruler. In the same way, the left brain has commandeered the right in order to reign over us and all we do, but with vastly limited perspective. The resultant disconnection, in which the left brain fails to share its feedback with the right, is a central pillar of the culture of absence in which we find ourselves. McGilchrist goes on to say: "Indeed, it is filled with an alarming self-confidence. My hope is that awareness of the situation may enable us to change course before it is too late."

This fundamental imbalance between doing and being generates a dangerously mechanistic and fragmented reality, one of disconnection and emptiness, in the face of which we often need tremendous quantities of power, money and possessions to cover the pain of the lack of belonging, the ache of disconnection.

The Leader as Healer actively cultivates the integration of being and doing, bringing together the whole brain, mind, body and heart into a single, coherent whole. Such leaders embody an inner operating system that is deeply rooted in being, so that their doing emerges as a highly attuned responsiveness to the needs of their environment, fit for the purpose of navigating the ever-increasing complexities and challenges of our time.

MEMO FROM A CEO CLIENT:

I always considered myself very good at reading the room – figuring out where people are coming from. Now, I recognize how my approach was a strictly mental or cognitive process, and therefore incomplete. Since that revelation, I've learned how to sense more deeply what people need instead of consciously analysing to figure them out.

Sometimes the signals I get about what's going on or what's needed in a situation don't actually make sense to me. But as I follow them through, I find out – perhaps a day or two later – that my approach was precisely what was needed, even if I wasn't clear on the reasons at the time. As a result, I have an easier time connecting with people, sensing what they need, and intuiting how best to move forwards so we can create a co-led journey as an organization.

When you're processing everything from the neck up, you're working to 'figure it all out,' as if everything's a puzzle piece or a move in a game of chess. You have to make it work, so you keep an eye on all the variables, but you actually miss so much. There is all of this profound intelligence in your body and in your spirit that you can learn to access.

A key part of my role today is simply staying open to all signals and messages — including those of a subtler variety — that can help me connect with the needs of all members of my team and with the broader society we are working to serve.

THE PRACTICE

Creating stable integration between being and doing takes practice. It is a path towards mastery. Along the way, you will find, as have countless practitioners before you, that you begin to navigate your days with much more efficiency and precision, and on many days, achieve far more, in far less time and with greater ease.

THE SIMPLEST, MOST POWERFUL TOOL WE HAVE IS OUR ATTENTION.

Learning to use our attention consciously and deliberately is the gateway through which we can relocate ourselves in being. The very act of paying attention draws us naturally and effortlessly back to a deep centre in ourselves, reawakens the right brain and begins to restore balance.

The good news is that attention is like a muscle: the more you use it, the stronger it gets. Even better news is that many cultures have spent thousands of years developing practices such as meditation and mindfulness, which demonstrably help grow and strengthen the capacities of awareness and attention. These techniques are now used effectively in prisons and in schools for students with behavioural problems, including issues of violence. Many organizations around the world are now embracing these practices for their members. (I explore this subject further in Chapter 5.)

The simple exercise described in the next few pages only takes a few minutes and will help you begin paying attention to your body and the environment around you. The suggestion at the end of the practice is an essential doorway to accessing and stabilizing the presence of Leader as Healer within. As simple as it seems, the challenge is to then instal the practice as a new habit. It can be helpful to set in place simple reminders: visual cues in your office space; timed reminders on your phone or computer calendar; perhaps an object kept in your pocket.

SOMATIC MINDFULNESS PRACTICE

Sit comfortably in your chair and either close your eyes or keep them open in very soft focus.

Pinch the top of one hand. Do this with either a light or firm pinch, but be sure to hold the pressure so that you can feel it distinctly.

Notice the sensation. Where is it? Is it just at the point you are pinching, or does the sensation spread? Does it feel hot or cold? Does it change as you breathe in or out?

Now, stop pinching. Notice how the sensation changes. Is there a feeling of instant relief? A tingling sensation? A feeling of numbness?

You have activated the function of attention.

Now, move your attention to your breath. What is the sensation of breathing in and out? What part of your body moves? Where do you feel your breath? How does the sensation change between the inhale and exhale? Perhaps you gradually notice more subtle sensations.

Move your awareness down the body to where it makes contact with the chair. Simply take notice of all the sensations of sitting.

Now, move your awareness gradually down your legs and gently focus your attention on the sensations of your feet and toes, including the point of contact between the soles of your feet and the floor.

Now, return your awareness to your breathing.

Gently include sound in your awareness. Do not strain to hear noises — just let them come to you. What can you hear? Notice any sounds as they float into your consciousness. See if you can detect still subtler sounds that you may not have noticed initially.

As you focus on sound, can you build an awareness of your breath again? Are you able to hold your attention on your body as you take notice of your senses and how they attune to the outside world?

Inner and outer attention, simultaneously.

After a few minutes, begin to think about coming out of the practice, and how it will be to maintain inner attention with your eyes open.

When you are ready, open your eyes. As you move through the day, try to maintain the quality of openness and sensing. Try staying attuned to your breathing, even as you begin to move and proceed through the day's tasks.

This is how to keep a small part of attention with you. You can come back to it at any time. If you feel yourself drifting in attention, simply come back to your breath.

CHAPTER 2

EMBRACING OUR EMOTIONS

When you think about companies with leaders who are deeply connected to their emotions, the auto industry probably doesn't leap to mind. The design, production and marketing of automobiles is highly complex and technical, and in fact many of the leaders in the industry move into management from engineering positions. Yet, even in seemingly unpromising soil, the emotional awareness and connection necessary to lead with presence can bloom.

I witnessed this first-hand while working with the senior leadership team of a major US automaker. The company was struggling to adapt to a rapidly changing and competitive landscape. Below the surface layer of rational discussion and debate, it was clear there was a lot of anxiety, even fear, about the future. After leading the group in a few cognitive exercises, I broke participants out into small groups and shifted their focus to emotions – namely, a discussion about fear, including the types and intensities of fear they were experiencing.

Initially (and unsurprisingly), the breakout groups struggled to respond. Eventually, they started leaning in and the atmosphere in the room palpably shifted, as it always does the moment people become less resistant and more open and present. In our subsequent debrief, participants spoke of how relieving and bonding it had been to speak so authentically with one another about vulnerable subject matter. One person then mentioned how, towards the end of the process, everyone seemed to have a flood of new ideas and insights about some of the more pressing challenges their organization was facing at the time. All around the room, heads were nodding. As we explored this together, everyone agreed that, rather than reverting to the habitual exile of tricky emotions like fear, each leader had simply made space for them.

Moreover, they experienced a profound insight: by opening up about and simply acknowledging their emotions together, new creative energies and ideas had begun to flow.

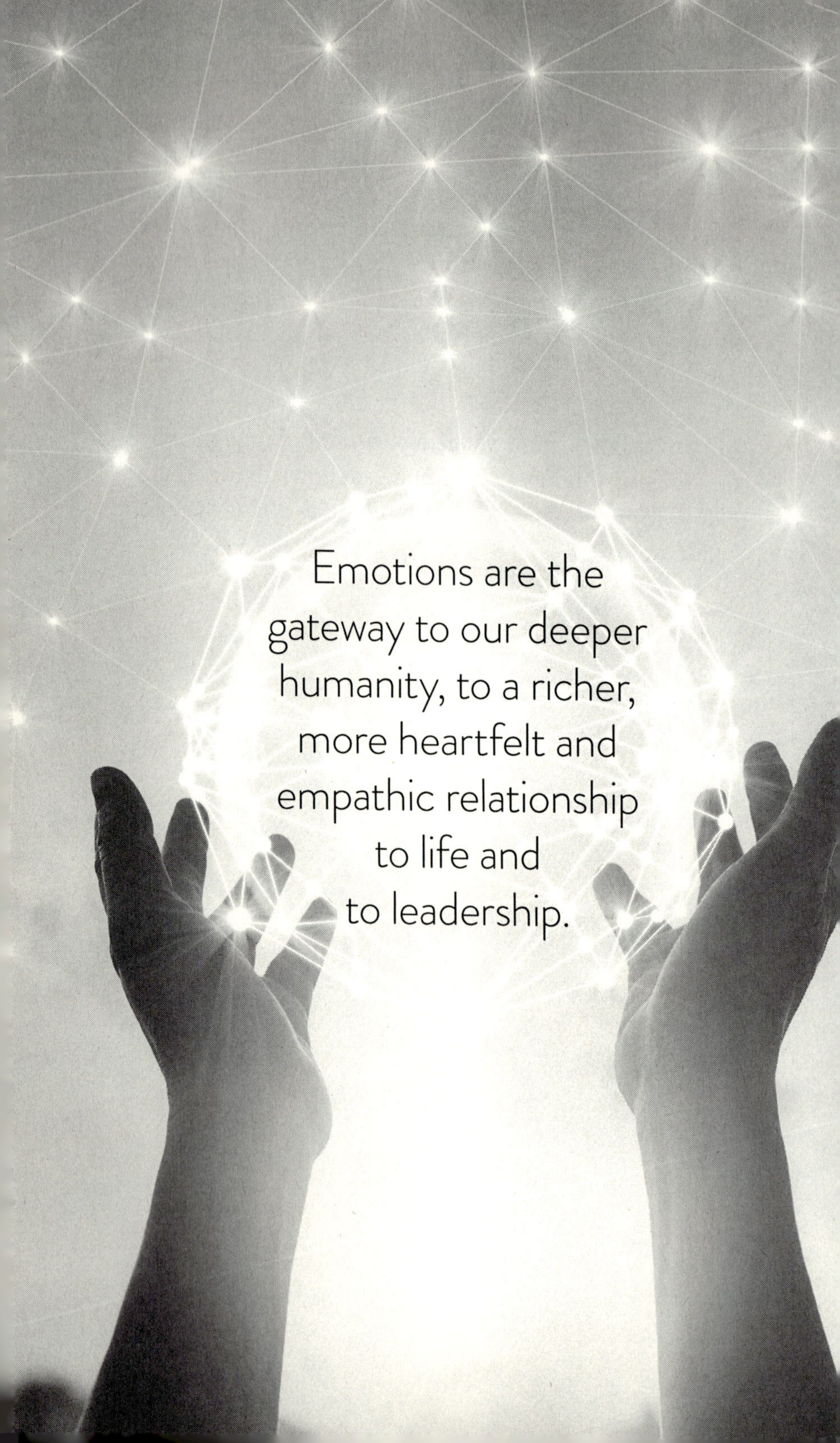
Emotions are the
gateway to our deeper
humanity, to a richer,
more heartfelt and
empathic relationship
to life and
to leadership.

THE PRINCIPLE

Emotions are the gateway to our deeper humanity. Connecting more consciously with our feeling states allows us a richer, more heartfelt and empathic relationship to life and to leadership. This in turn heightens energy and connectedness, which provide the foundation for higher levels of perception, vision, insight and innovation.

The way we relate to – or, more often, do not relate to – our emotions is one of the biggest sources of fragmentation and disconnectedness in our culture. Yet, this challenge presents a ripe opportunity for change. By facing it, leaders can cross a prime transformational gateway towards bringing deeper presence and coherence to themselves and their organizations.

When was the last time you sobbed as you watched the news? How do you respond when presented with shocking images of people suffering? Does your mind simply filter them as just more data, without processing the emotions involved? When was the last time you felt heartbroken as you witnessed the ways we are destroying our planet, or felt stunned by the number of living species that are disappearing as a result of human greed and carelessness?

I am not suggesting that we become distressed and overwhelmed by the news on a daily basis. Rather, I believe it essential to recognize the state of collective numbness that has enveloped us, and how much it has become normalized. The consequence of this widespread numbing of emotion is that it has significantly eroded our capacity to care and connect. The inability to feel and embrace our emotions distances us from life itself, and results in a gradual freezing of the human heart. This 'absencing' of the heart impoverishes our lives, our leadership competency, and culture at large.

As the author, Buddhist scholar and environmental activist Joanna Macy states, "We are capable of suffering with our world, and that is the true meaning of compassion. It enables us to recognize our profound interconnectedness with all beings. Don't ever apologize for crying for the trees burning in the Amazon or over the waters polluted from mines in the Rockies. Don't apologize for the sorrow, grief and rage you feel. It is a measure of your humanity and your maturity. It is a measure of your open heart, and as your heart breaks open there will be room for the world to heal. That is what is happening as we see people honestly confronting the sorrows of our time."

The Leader as Healer is committed to bringing body, mind and heart together. In the previous chapter, we explored the foundational principles of being and doing. In this chapter, we bring emotions to the table. This is an essential part of the work of any Leader as Healer.

REWRITING YOUR MINDSET

Many cultures and the organizations within them have developed two false beliefs about human emotions. The first is that there is such a thing as 'positive' and 'negative' emotion. The second is that emotions make us weak, unpredictable and ultimately unproductive.

Ask yourself: Do you believe that fear blocks you? If your answer is yes, you are not alone. Whenever I put this question to a room full of executives, virtually all agree that fear is an obstacle. The prevailing belief is that we should block out or otherwise rid ourselves of fear, since sitting in this 'negative' emotion prevents us from taking the bold steps required to solve problems.

But nothing could be further from the truth.

What blocks our ability to solve problems is the act of *blocking the feeling of fear itself*. Once someone feels safe enough to allow the feeling of fear – to relax and pay attention first to the physical sensations of fear, and only secondarily to the thought patterns and narratives it creates – there is almost always a moment of shift or opening. This usually leads to an energizing or settling sensation, felt throughout the body, which is the exact opposite of being stuck or blocked.

The particular way that we inhibit our emotions was initially learned in childhood, within our family. What emotions were welcomed in your family? How did others respond when you felt sad or frightened or angry? Were your feelings listened to and validated? Or were you told not to cry, not to get so excited, not to feel?

Every senior leader I have met, however skilled, successful or powerful, carries an unattended package of emotional scars, hurts and fears. Most of its contents originate in childhood and can include anything from minor indignities to severe adversity and trauma. Children feel all such experiences intensely and physically. Without the support of an open and attuned parent or caregiver, the child's nervous system cannot digest difficult experiences and intense emotions. In an effort to inhibit fear and pain, the muscles of the body become tense, the heart rate rises, or breathing becomes shallow. This autonomic survival response is the body packing away difficult feelings in order to simply move on. Indeed, we all learned early on how to lock difficult emotions in a dark cellar outside conscious awareness and to simply live on as if they were not there.

Fear has never blocked us.
What blocks us is our inability to
actually *feel* the fear. The Leader
as Healer knows that by simply
acknowledging and meeting
emotions without condition
a profound alchemy of relaxation
and connection can occur.

This was an essential survival mechanism, and it is remarkable how we instinctively knew how to do this.

But, try as we might, and however much we may wish otherwise, we see that in our adulthood these fragmented experiences and painful emotions do not stay locked away without consequence. The frozen blocks of energy within show themselves as limiting symptoms in our lives, often compromising our vitality, reducing our ability to relate to others, and interrupting our capacity to be truly present. Furthermore, buried and unresolved emotions limit and distort our critical thinking faculty, the very thing we so highly prize.

The exiling of emotion is one of the foundational pillars of a culture of absence. The process has become so normalized that we are blind to the degree to which it narrows our range of perception and underpins the domination of the rational mind.

The act of suppressing emotions is neither conscious nor malicious. In fact, many times we suppress emotions out of a misplaced desire to protect someone else from discomfort or pain. Consider a time when someone you love was deeply sad. Your reflex may have been to try and 'fix' the problem for them, or somehow help to make their pain 'go away.' In truth, this sort of response was very likely more about diminishing your own discomfort. So long as we have exiled our own emotions, it is much harder to just sit with someone in pain, to simply be with them and allow them the space to fully feel their experience. To say, *I am here*. When someone is allowed to feel sadness or pain or fear in the presence of an empathic, non-interfering person, they nearly always experience relief, and often come away with a new sense for how to navigate their current challenge. Every one of us shares the simple and profound need to be heard, to be received, from the moment of our conception to the moment we die.

KEY MESSAGE:
STOP TRYING TO 'FIX' EMOTIONS.

The Leader as Executor endorses disconnection, encouraging us to ignore our emotions in order to get on with the tasks at hand. The Leader as Healer knows that by simply acknowledging and meeting emotions without condition, a profound alchemy of relaxation and connection can occur. This recognition is an essential part of the maturity that emerges from the more developed consciousness of Leader as Healer.

As the psychotherapist and poet Miriam Greenspan states in *Healing Through the Dark Emotions:* "Vulnerability is at the heart of our human capacity for empathy; for suffering, but also for joy; for hurt, but also for compassion; for loneliness, but also for connection. When we are most vulnerable, we are most alive, most open to all the dimensions of existence. In our vulnerability is our power."[12]

THE LANGUAGE OF EMOTION

When most of us are asked how we are feeling, we usually reply instead with what we are *thinking*. Most of us habitually minimize or skip over our true feeling states and launch directly into analysis, rationalization and reasoning, without taking an opportunity to really feel and share. It is important to recognize these patterns and learn to precisely discern the differences between thought and emotion. To do so, we have to learn to *slow down*, otherwise our speedy minds always take over.

By deconstructing common beliefs about emotion, the Leader as Healer finds a way to clarify, enhance and repair emotional disconnection. He or she understands that there are no positive or negative emotions. All are simply an expression of our natural life energy, and therefore an essential part of our humanity. The 'repair' happens through feeling, not through changing anything. This is simple, and radical. When we start to work with ourselves in this domain, we discover the myriad strategies we all have for moving away from actually feeling an emotion. These have built over many years. They have been needed self-protection. When we are ready, we start to allow some of the self-protection to melt. As we do so, whole parts of us come back 'online,' as if we had taken the USB connector out, and now we plug it back in.

A client who leads a large corporation in the United States once eloquently explained his own fragmentation. He said that he recognized his tendency to compartmentalize or 'cut off' various parts of himself, particularly his emotions, in an attempt to fit into what he believed were acceptable moulds, and in order to get where he was in the corporate world.

"That was all fine because it was required — or seemed to be required — at the time," he said. "But when you come out the other end, if you can't reclaim all the pieces of yourself, you're left hobbling out the door."

THE EMOTIONAL LANDSCAPE

There are four primary human emotions: fear, anger, joy and sadness. A bit like the artist's colour wheel, each of these primary emotions can be thought of as residing on a spectrum, and each can blend with the others to form many shades. Fear, for example, can range from mild anxiety to naked terror; sadness from mild upset to deep grief. When we feel safe enough to truly feel our emotions, they become energy that flows through us, relaxing the body, grounding us deeply within ourselves, and often opening higher channels of insight and creativity.

But, when any emotion is blocked, we are left cold and numb. Without being able to feel sad we will never be able to feel joy. By feeling and processing our emotions, we move through to the other side, where we experience greater peace. We acquire greater access to the heart, and experience more tenderness, openness and compassion for ourselves and others. And this broadens our operating bandwidth by uniting logic, discernment and analysis with greater embodiment and emotional depth.

Inner work is required to learn to attend to the hidden wounds we carry within. For this, we have to go down into the cellar. The client mentioned above uses the analogy of yoga to explain this process. In yoga, we learn a series of postures that are difficult at first, but eventually become second nature. The body learns to breathe and flow from one movement into the next. In the process, we sometimes experience an injury that makes our movements more difficult and requires that we patiently isolate each muscle in order to find the knot or tension, so that we can work with it. The same is true in the process of reconnecting with the emotions; when we encounter difficult and ingrained emotional responses, we are called to isolate the injury and ease out the knots.

This should be done in a safe relational space, the kind that can be provided by a compassionate friend or colleague, or with the help of a skilled guide, attuned coach or therapist, who will not try to fix or over analyse. Often, the simple action of acknowledging an emotion can bring a sense of transformational release. And the Leader as Healer is committed to the work, in order to develop the maturity that can create the conditions for genuine emotional intelligence to flourish in the organization.

I have witnessed hundreds of instances in which, by simply hearing and acknowledging an emotion, a person experienced an opening to new possibilities of movement and resolution, far beyond what are arrived at through the automatic impulse to 'fix' a given problem. More often than not, an individual actually arrives at a solution after feeling heard and received.

Indeed, I have provided space for many senior executives as they engaged with their emotions, remaining present and attuned to them as they sobbed or experienced their fear or anger more fully. This process creates a powerful release, after which the person feels much more settled and relaxed. Many expressed that they'd been waiting years to simply be allowed to feel.

In reconnecting with emotions, the Leader as Healer is able to navigate the world with heart and empathy. They show up more fully, and with a greater sense of attunement to themselves and others. All good leaders, like top sports coaches, know naturally how to speak to every person differently. This is a key leadership competency. Poor leaders address everyone according to their own mood, because they have little capacity for real attunement to another person. How can they, when they are not attuned to themselves?

The more present and open I become, the better able I am to feel what is happening emotionally in *you*. When I can feel your interior emotional landscape, I receive much more information about the needs, desires and motivations that drive your behaviour. And, if I am able to sensitively and accurately articulate what you may be feeling then, together, we share a moment of relating in which you can feel me feeling you, and vice versa. This creates a powerful connection that goes far beyond the transactional relationships we have been conditioned to engage in. And with greater connection, we can achieve a higher level of resolution.

Indeed, this is how we break through emotional absence. In this process, it is critical that we learn to be precise about our emotions; finding the right word for a feeling creates a powerful synchronization between mind, body and heart. One of the most common patterns of disconnection is reflected in the simple words: 'I feel that...' A sentence beginning with those words will always be a thought, not a feeling. An accurate response to the question 'How are you feeling?' begins with 'I feel...' followed by one variation or combination of the four primary emotions.

When asked how I am feeling, if I slow down enough to check carefully, I might respond this way: 'Well, I notice a kind of numbness inside me,' or, 'I feel some tension in my stomach. And as I bring my awareness to it, I sense a feeling of anxiety.' Sometimes, we feel equanimity and calm; we feel present and connected without any strong emotions. Other times, we recognize some emotion, but find that it is surrounded by fog. As we learn to be patient and precise in the process, we discover how powerful it is to stop fixing and start being with whatever is present.

Sometimes, you might feel a mix of emotions, or discover that one emotion is covering another — very often, anger conceals grief or fear. This tendency is strongly influenced by culture: men frequently feel anger but have more difficulty acknowledging the underlying fear or sadness. Women, on the other hand, are often able to feel sadness but not always the anger that may underpin it. In this way, both men and women lose access to the substantial store of life energy and power that are latent within their buried and suppressed emotions.

I have worked with many senior women executives who expressed frustration that, whenever they are seething with anger, they start to cry. The notion that 'nice girls don't get angry' is deeply ingrained in our cultural condition and is just as limiting as the idea that 'real men don't cry and should feel no fear.'

The importance of linguistic precision is recognized in developmental psychology. If a child is having a tantrum and an adult says, 'You are feeling x or y,' but 'x' or 'y' is incorrect – or the wrong word has been used to identify the emotion – the child's behaviour will often escalate. But, when a loving caregiver finds the right word for the emotion that child is feeling, the child will feel seen and understood. This provides a sense of security and relaxation, and the situation is diffused. Mind, body and heart can then settle into a state of coherence.

The same principle applies in organizational leadership. Leaders as Healer have learned to work with their own inner emotional landscapes, which allows them to hold unconditional space for others' emotions. No drama necessary; just simple, accurate acknowledgement.

During a retreat I held for chief executives in the United States, one participant had a 'lightbulb moment.' He recalled an incident in which he had discovered an employee engaging in illegal activity and called the police.

"They came first thing in the morning," said the executive, "and, in front of everyone in our open plan office, handcuffed the man and marched him out. Staff were understandably shocked. Later in the morning, I called everyone together, explained why I had involved the police, and encouraged everyone to get on with their work."

But, for the rest of the day and most of that week, he explained, people were in "a kind of daze."

> In his 'lightbulb' moment, he realized that an alternative approach would have been better. He could have instead called everyone together and said something like: "I'm angry at our long-term colleague for committing this crime, but I'm also shocked and upset to have seen him arrested in front of us. And, I imagine many of you may be feeling similarly, so let's take a moment just to acknowledge the mix of emotions we're all feeling. Take a few minutes to turn to the person next to you, and share how you are both doing."
>
> "Had I done that," he said, "had I simply acknowledged how everyone was feeling, we would have saved hundreds of hours of sub-par performance."

Staff meetings can be transformed when a leader has sufficient maturity and inner capacity to invite a pause and openly acknowledges their own feelings, such as a sense of anxiety while in the middle of a challenging project. This kind of acknowledgement affords permission to everyone else in the room who is feeling similarly to acknowledge it. There is no need for judgement, over-analysis or drama. No need to 'fix it.' It need only take a few minutes, yet the strategic discussion that continues afterwards will almost certainly be of a much higher quality, because the individual and group 'body' have stopped fighting the anxiety.

This next point is key: those who possess emotional maturity do not react, but instead *respond*. They are able to respond well because they can feel and relate with others. The truth is that simple: unconditional acknowledgement of our emotional realities obviates the potential for blaming, mudslinging or other unwelcome outbursts. It is, therefore, just wise practice. When teams learn these 'skills' they invariably transition into powerful new levels of engagement, energy and creative thinking.

One of my chief executive clients leads a large organization and simultaneously holds several board positions. He recently reflected on his experience being in a board meeting of a major US company in which a deeply heartfelt conversation occurred. Members spent the meeting discussing the idea that everyone's humanity 'needed to shine.' At some point in the course of that meeting, he said, everyone present had shed a tear.

"I had never been in a board meeting where anything like that had happened," he said. "Not ever. And I bet it has never happened in any Fortune 50 company before!"

A little while later, he wrote to me: "Just had our company board meeting. Everybody was in the usual strategic planning mode. Then, I asked the question, 'How is the leadership team feeling?' It was a cathartic conversation, and something completely different opened up."

Never say never.

The Leader as Healer embodies what poet David Whyte calls 'robust vulnerability' – the ability to be fully present with their own emotions without becoming overwhelmed. Such leaders foster organizational cultures in which emotions are acknowledged as an innate and essential aspect of our humanity. Disallowing vulnerability by concealing or rushing to solve it belongs to a dying paradigm. The great irony of that former worldview is that, in trying to model 'strength,' the pathway to true power and insight is blocked. The so-called strength is one-dimensional, based on suppression and a small, insecure ground of identity.

When I work with leaders and with teams, we focus together on gently melting the barriers we have erected around emotions. We seek a willingness to unconditionally meet whatever emotions are present, to sit with discomfort if need be, and we find that the practice creates real interconnection. At a fundamental level, this process allows us to rewrite the cultural code and thereby release massive amounts of new, creative, purposeful energy. The willingness to authentically engage in such work is the essence of maturity.

Some years ago, I worked with the UK Permanent Secretaries, the highest level of the civil service. One PS shared a salient story. He had recently been interviewed for the evening news, during which he mentioned that he had not been sleeping well due to a challenging, multi-million-pound initiative.

Afterwards, the PS worried that perhaps he shouldn't have been so honest. Yet, when he went into work the next morning, he was surprised by how many of his colleagues made a point of telling him they were grateful for what he had shared. By discussing his difficulty openly, the PS had legitimized their own concerns.

As a result, he said, everyone seemed to bring a greater sense of availability and connection to their work on the difficult initiative.

Another gave a perfect example of the power of simply acknowledging emotion. Working with a new minister on a challenging, big-budget initiative, their relationship was full of tension and never-ending fighting. One day, as they were walking to a meeting along the river near Parliament in London, he mentioned that this project was keeping him awake at night. The minister stopped walking, looked him directly in the eye and said: "I am so glad to hear you say that. I have never felt so challenged, and am living with an almost constant background anxiety about this project."

In that simple exchange, their relationship was completely transformed.

Vulnerability is our natural underlying condition. Our choice is whether to deny it or embrace it. As David Whyte states: "Vulnerability is not a weakness, a passing indisposition, or something we can arrange to do without, vulnerability is not a choice, vulnerability is the underlying, ever present and abiding undercurrent of our natural state."

He continues: "To run from vulnerability is to run from the essence of our nature, the attempt to be invulnerable is the vain attempt to become something we are not, and most especially, to close off our understanding of the grief of others. More seriously, in refusing our vulnerability we refuse to ask for the help needed at every turn of our existence and immobilize the essential, tidal and conversational foundations of our identity.

"To have a temporary, isolated sense of power over all events and circumstances is a lovely, illusory privilege and perhaps the prime beautifully constructed conceit of being human and most especially of being youthfully human, but it is a privilege that must be surrendered with that same youth, with ill health, with accident, with the loss of loved ones who do not share our untouchable powers, powers eventually and most emphatically given up, as we approach our last breath.

"The only choice we have as we mature is how we inhabit our vulnerability, how we become larger and more courageous and more compassionate through our intimacy with disappearance, our choice is to inhabit vulnerability as generous citizens of loss, robustly and fully, or conversely, as misers and complainers, reluctant, and fearful, always at the gates of existence, but never bravely and completely attempting to enter, never wanting to risk ourselves, never walking fully through the door."[13]

Perhaps you worry that by attuning to colleagues, particularly in a one-to-one setting, you may start to take on their problems. Thankfully, this is neither the aim nor the result. The Leader as Healer does not take on others' emotions. When it comes to working with other people, staying emotionally open allows you to connect to them so that you can better understand and acknowledge how they feel – nothing more, at least not if you are well grounded. The other person is able to feel you feeling them, and simple empathic acknowledgement is all that is needed to help unblock the energy and arrive at their own solutions.

In the end, as Brené Brown says in *Dare to Lead*: "Leaders must either invest a reasonable amount of time attending to fears and feelings or squander an unreasonable amount of time trying to manage ineffective and unproductive behaviour."[14]

Becoming comfortable with the world of emotions is therefore a deep and essential part of the work of the Leader as Healer. It transforms our capacity to co-create the organizational cultures in which energy and connection flow freely, so that higher levels of potential, insight and innovation can be awakened and tapped.

COLLECTIVE AND INTER-GENERATIONAL IMPRINTS

The subject of collective trauma[15] and intergenerational wounds is far deeper and more complex than can be explored here, but all leaders who desire to work towards their highest potential should have at least some familiarity with them.

Some of the unattended scars we carry originated long before we were born, while others were brought to us through the wider historical and cultural landscape that surrounds us. Unresolved trauma may be rooted in past natural disasters, social conflict, crime, systemic inequality, or that most pervasive of traumatizing injuries: man's inhumanity to man. Whatever its origins, the imprint of human suffering affects us all in some way, often more than we realize.

Startling new research into the effects of collective trauma is being carried out across the scientific community, particularly in the field of epigenetics. Put simply, epigenetics is the study of how gene expression is modified by certain external effects, although it is important to know that the genetic code itself is not altered. Significant stress or illness, for example, may supress or 'turn off' the expression of certain genes or 'turn on' the expression of others.

Epigenetic researchers at the University of Zürich carried out studies on the impact of stress and adversity in a species of mice. Their research revealed that the consequences of shock or distress in male mice were actually passed down to their generational descendants via epigenetic markers to the DNA (carried in the sperm), even though the subject males had no subsequent social interaction or other contact with their progeny. In fact, the impact of these epigenetic markers for stress were observed in the next *four* generations of mice (despite these mice themselves being subjected to no adverse or stressful conditions) and could be seen outwardly in behavioural traits such as higher instances of agitation, anxiety and fear.[16]

We know that this is also true for humans. Studies of Holocaust survivors and their descendants, for example, have repeatedly revealed the transgenerational nature of trauma.[17] It is not just those who experience direct trauma who are forced to bear its weight; children and grandchildren frequently express the consequences of a forebear's traumatic experiences, even when the trauma in question was never spoken of among family or the community.

In fact, the silence in many ways compounds the trauma. Wherever there are communities that endured (but did not heal from) historical trauma, we frequently observe higher rates of many diseases, greater instances of early death, mental illness, addiction and other limiting social problems. These are just some of the many consequences of unattended historical and generational suffering.

In order to understand the complicated emotional and behavioural patterns that trauma leaves behind, we must be willing to look beyond personal biography, or rather, to expand our thinking to realize that biography is never entirely personal but is instead shared with and influenced by culture. The life of the individual is necessarily formed and informed by his or her familial, communal and sociocultural experience. Full stop.

The point is this: disharmonious and unhealthy patterns from the past continue to repeat in our lives, however unconsciously, until they are brought fully into awareness and space is made for healing. Whatever hurts or wounds our ancestors were unable to resolve in their own lifetimes are bequeathed to us. As a wise client once said: "Hurts are passed down through the generations until someone is ready to feel them." This is why the unconditional willingness to sit with physical and emotional sensations is so important. It is the critical work that allows us to thaw the frozen aspects of the past in order to make present what has been absent.

Hurts are passed down
through the generations
until someone is ready
to feel them.

THE PRACTICE

On the next few pages are some simple reflective practices that can help us initiate the transformational journey of attuning more deeply to ourselves and others; a foundational competency for all Leaders as Healer.

REFLECTION EXERCISE

Consider your relationship to each of the core emotions — fear, anger, joy and sadness — in the following contexts:

- When you are alone, which of these emotions do you allow yourself to feel? (It may be all, a combination, or none.)
- Which of these core emotions do you allow other people to see in you? Which do you hide?
- How do you relate to others when they are expressing these emotions? Do you try to fix the situation? Or, are you able to stay present and open in the face of these emotions?
- How would you describe your capacity for intimacy? How close do you let others come to you, or how closely do you engage with others?
- How much do you feel within you what is happening inside other people? How perceptive are you at noticing what is happening emotionally in others?

ACTION STEPS TO DEVELOP YOUR EMOTIONAL CAPACITY

Start to pay closer attention to your emotional life.

- Keep a journal and write down your observations about what you felt in different situations, particularly in those that precipitate or accompany difficulty or stress. (For example, what were your emotions during that board meeting? How did those emotions change at different points?)

Find at least one or two people who are committed to being more emotionally attuned and who share an understanding that emotions do not need to be fixed.

- Meet with these people regularly, in person or by video call

- Choose a recent situation or relationship that you are finding difficult. It can be personal or professional. Practice creating an unconditionally safe listening space for each other in which you are allowed to feel and express each emotional layer involved

- Go slowly and support each other in the effort to stop escaping feelings by moving into thinking
- If someone says, "I don't know what I am feeling," or "I feel numb," simply honour and respect this

Every once in a while, go sit in a café. Look around discreetly. Without hearing the words being spoken, develop your capacity to attune to the emotional strata of the people and encounters you witness. Notice any insecurities, sadness, irritation or numbness — the many layers of humanity below the surface of human interaction.

CHAPTER 3

THE POWER OF EMBODIMENT

On the second day of a programme I led in 2019, a senior Saudi Arabian executive approached me during the break. “In the last several months,” he said, “I’ve been feeling overweight and generally bad about my body. After our work on reconnecting with the body yesterday, I felt something different. Today, I went to do my morning prayer as usual, and as I stood in the first position, I had a completely new and direct experience of my body. And a deeper sense of its purpose, as well as the precise reason for this position, and of the nature of prayer itself... this, after 40 years of daily praying!”

It is remarkable when a profound insight can flow from such a simple exercise, and quite startling that so few leaders actually undertake such work. The exercise the leader experienced was a deceptively modest one that almost always generates deep discovery and connection. It involved a simple but structured process of connecting to one’s breath and grounding the body. This is combined with attentional focus, which puts it at the beginning of a ‘relocation.’ And then, by the time the exercise is finished, most people experience a very strong inner connectedness and ease. Through regular practice, the exercise begins to rewire certain neuropathways. Sometimes, the effects are immediately profound, as was the case for the executive from Saudi Arabia.

THE PRINCIPLE

The body is your primary gateway to a sense of aliveness. It is also the conduit through which you can access multiple layers of perception, information and inner knowing. When your relationship to the body is nurtured, you experience a deep sense of being 'at home' in yourself and in the world.

Even if you have lost a fuller connection to your body over time, you perhaps remember what it felt like to be a child, when life was an intensely *physical* experience, moment-to-moment.

As adults, we are more likely to experience a sense of disconnection from the body. This disconnection is another normalized pillar of a culture of absence. Dissociation is another way of describing disembodiment. When we disassociate from our emotions and bodily sensations, we abandon ourselves in a fundamental way.

Disassociation shuts down a primary channel of the nervous system, leaving us access to only a limited part of who we are. The result is that we cannot be fully present and available.

And we can feel the same disconnection in others. For example, when a leader we work with is ungrounded and disembodied, we instinctively feel less safe in their presence. Restoring connection to the body – becoming more embodied, present and available – is therefore an essential part of the work of any Leader as Healer.

We are all born embodied, a natural experience for healthy humans. The rift that we later experience between mind and body is something we learn.

As a child, you likely had very physical interactions with the world: living moment-to-moment and feeling every sensation of your body and emotions. This is an optimum, natural state. However, disassociation and disembodiment are not pathological; they arise as an intelligent survival response to adversity and trauma, as we saw in the previous chapter. As children, we have many experiences that we cannot process right away, or even for a while afterwards. These range from seemingly small moments in which we felt alone and unsupported to more extreme abuse scenarios. We have to close down as a matter of survival. We do this by tensing the body and restricting our breathing. In more extreme circumstances, we effectively leave our body altogether. By shutting down how we feel in those experiences, we preserve the energetic and cognitive resources needed just to get through them. When shutting down becomes a long-term pattern, however – when those experiences never get processed or resolved – we become removed from ourselves and from one another.

The body/mind divide is then compounded by family, community and society. Western educational systems and other institutions prioritize reason and logic, and reward (or punish) members on that basis. Ask yourself: When you were in school, how much emphasis was placed on creativity versus knowledge? How much emphasis on play versus data? Today's school children are increasingly tested on their ability to recall facts and calculate logical operations, while physical and creative activities are deemphasized or underfunded in favour of knowledge accumulation. This way of teaching and learning gradually divides us from the body and the inner self, creating a chasm of separation within. There are many powerful voices calling for this to be redressed.[18] The pandemic has led to home schooling on screens, and then mask-wearing classrooms, which can only have compounded the fracture.

Our bodies keep us connected to ourselves and to the world around us. Our physical senses allow us to explore, understand and feel alive. They allow us to detect and decode multiple sources of information from the environment. We can see in every indigenous culture a remarkable richness of connection with nature, felt through the body, a reminder of just how much we have lost through our hyper-rationalization. And our bodies channel energy; when open and connected, we are better able to ground ourselves, and to understand and connect with others.

Emotion is dependent on the flow of energy through the human body. When we block our emotions, we do so by holding tension in the body so that emotional energy is blocked and prevented from moving through us. This breaks our internal sense of connection or flow and disembodies us. But when we allow ourselves to feel, without judgement or opinion, we permit the flow of energy through the body and we feel more energized and alive, and much clearer in our thinking. It is how we are supposed to be.

In my work, I frequently sit with my clients as they experience difficult emotions. Afterwards, they report feeling more aware of their bodies – particularly the legs – and more grounded and alive. Put simply: by connecting with our emotions, we experience greater embodiment. The two are inextricably interconnected. And this allows us to feel more at home in ourselves and in the world.

The body is your primary
gateway to a sense of aliveness.
It is also the conduit through
which you can access multiple
layers of perception,
information and inner knowing.

Many clients realize that what they used to believe was 'reading a room' and working out where people are coming from was a primarily rational process and that, following our work together, rather than constantly analysing people, they get much more subtle and accurate information through their sensing capacities.

As one CEO said to me: "Sometimes the signals I get about what's going on or what is needed in a situation won't even make sense to me. But I'll follow it through and find out a day or two later that I'd picked up precisely what was needed at that time, even if I wasn't clear about the reasons."

Consider those moments when you have felt most relaxed and in touch with your body. Your breathing felt freer, your senses more open, and you felt more at ease in the world. Perhaps you experience this when you are in nature, just after a workout, when playing sports, or simply when relaxing. Whatever the case, you feel more centred, present and 'at home' in yourself. If you practice yoga, Qigong or a martial art, you will certainly have felt this quite regularly. The world feels palpably different after a really good class: the sights, sounds and smells around you are more vivid, more energized.

In his book, *Touching Enlightenment*, the American Buddhist academic Reginald Ray writes: "When we begin to inhabit the body as a primary way of sensing, feeling and knowing the world, then we find that we as human beings are in a state of intimate relationship and connection with all that is."[19]

But to what degree is this your home base throughout the day? What percentage of the time do you experience this aliveness, this embodiment? When I pose this question to a group of executives, there is usually a sense of shock to realize that the average time is around 5%. The Leader as Healer understands that this need not be the case; that this is an aberration we have normalized, and that it can and must be transformed.

FEEDBACK FROM A SENIOR MEMBER OF ONE OF THE UK'S MAIN INTELLIGENCE AGENCIES AFTER A THREE-DAY RETREAT WITH THE TOP TEAM:

"There have been many transformational benefits in myself and the team. One of the most palpable is how much more embodied I feel throughout the day. It may sound strange, but this has literally given me a new inner home, one in which I have so much more energy and, even more importantly, a far wider perceptual capacity. I'm quite sure that my strategic thinking mind is functioning at a higher level now that it has become a part of me, rather than the centre of who I am or thought I was.

"Why wasn't I taught this at the beginning of my career?!"

Artistic performance is a powerful reminder of embodiment. One week, you might go to the theatre to see Shakespeare's *Hamlet* and find yourself painfully bored for four hours. Go another time, when there are different actors, and you may find yourself electrified, hanging on every line and scene. The latter likely happened because the actors were at one with their bodies and, therefore, inhabited the emotions of their characters. Their entire performance, the words and actions they portray on stage, was aligned with their own energy and, as such, enraptured you. It is the same with dancers and musicians. Think of the difference it makes for you when a singer truly connects to the lyrics and expresses depth and emotion through a song. Embodiment is one of the greatest gifts of any performer, and one we all instinctively crave.

The American rock singer Joan Osborne said: "A lot of times when I'm on stage, I'll get covered in goose bumps. I'll start to feel this pleasure in just breathing, and the singing is suddenly completely effortless. It's something I feel in my skin and all up and down my body. That happens a lot. It's a personal thing, but it also feels like I'm being part of something larger."[20]

The Leader as Healer prioritizes reunification with the body. They understand that embodiment ignites a sense of aliveness, creates space and availability for others, and reaffirms our connection to the world. This generates a sense of grounded presence, a quality that says, *"I am here, and I am available."* Other people can sense it, and because they do, it increases shared presence and connection. Additionally, embodiment enhances our senses, allowing us to pick up subtler signals and signs, and therefore deepens our intuition. It allows for a blend of reason and emotion, and fosters a higher level of consciousness and a more sophisticated response to opportunities and challenges.

The rational mind alone is no longer enough; we have forgotten the deep wisdom of the body, and it is now time to resurrect it.

I have a good friend who has won many international awards and been nominated three times for the Nobel Peace Prize. Keen to understand her inner process, I asked her once how she approaches very difficult scenarios. You may find her answer surprising: "I use my meditation practice to quieten down internally," she said. "Then, I move my awareness slowly and precisely down to my womb. After a short time, wise responses almost always emerge."

There is an important lesson in what my friend shared: if we are to thrive in an increasingly complex and uncertain world, we must bring all of ourselves to the problem-solving table. To do that, we must represent an embodied, coherent whole. The rational mind alone is no longer enough; we have forgotten the deep wisdom of the body, and it is now time to resurrect it.

SOMETIMES THIS IS SIMPLE AND IMMEDIATELY TRANSFORMATIONAL.

> At the beginning of the second day of a programme, a Dubai CEO wanted to tell us all something about his experience of embodiment: "Last night, I was in my hotel room and saw that my Chairman was calling. We have a tense and often fractious relationship. Remembering our work yesterday, I took a couple of deep breaths and grounded myself strongly in my body. The result? We had the best conversation we have ever had."
>
> Yes, it can be that simple. Try doing that before every Zoom meeting. You will soon see the difference in your state, and therefore your availability.

Another time I asked the writer of a dozen successful novels, with a daily writing practice of at least six hours, how he knew that his writing on any particular day was in the 'zone' of high creativity. He thought for a moment and then said: "Because my breathing changes..."

Over the years, I have asked many senior leaders how they make their most important decisions. More than 90% report that they carefully analyse all available data, and then go by their 'gut feeling' – a term we use to refer to the body's sense of knowing, or instinct. Wherever reason and sensing (doing and being) come together, we experience greater and more coherent processing capacity.

The essence of the Leader as Healer is a truly embodied person who can balance reason and intuition; logic and senses; receptivity and proactivity. It is someone who possesses grounded presence and attunement, for themselves and others.

MEMO FROM A CEO CLIENT ON THE PROCESS OF AWAKENING TO THE POWER OF EMBODIMENT:

When I used to go home at night, there were reverberations and mini earthquakes in my psyche because you're not actually working it all through. It just kind of stays stuck. And you don't even realize you're doing it. Five or ten years into the process, you don't even realize that's what you're doing. You become disembodied because you're only able to kind of access your mental capacity, and almost everything else is deadened and not available as processing capacity.

I still remember in the first few months of working with Nicholas when I started to notice that I would have chills down my spine. I mean, that's a very common reaction. Everyone can probably remember a time when they were having a conversation with someone or they hear something, and it sends chills down their spine. But I had not registered that reaction to anything in probably decades before that time. And that's a primal, innate intelligence that is telling you something very important to how you see the world or move through the world that I now realize is almost impossible to live without. And, yet, I had so disembodied myself that I had forgotten that was even a reaction my body could have.

When you are processing everything from the neck up, you're trying to figure it out like everything's a puzzle and a piece, and you're going to figure out the chess game, and you're going to make it work, and you're going to keep your eye on all the variables. But you miss so much because you have all of this intelligence in your body and in your spirit that you are closed to.

PHYSICAL HEALTH

With disembodiment, on the other hand, we observe negative physical and other effects: the rational mind takes over and we go from the alignment of this:

To the distortion of this:

In fact, disembodiment can actually lead to physical pain and chronic health problems, including:

JOINT PAIN. Chronic poor posture can result in a misalignment of vital joints, placing added strain on vulnerable areas like the knees, for example. Over the long term, increased pressure can damage the joints, causing pain and potentially aggravating issues like arthritis.[21]

BACK PAIN. One of the most common symptoms of poor posture is chronic back pain, caused by increased pressure on the spine. Over time, it can contribute to disc degeneration, in which the vital discs between the spinal vertebrae wear down from the strain and become inflamed and painful.

POOR CIRCULATION. Slumped over a desk all day, blood cannot circulate as freely as it should through the body. Over time, this can contribute to varicose and spider veins – swollen, purplish-blue veins that can be painful and unsightly.[22]

PINCHED NERVES. Persistent poor posture may lead to a slight shift in the skeletal system and misalignment of the spine. This can create pinched nerves and result in numbness or pain in many parts of the body, including the back, arms, legs, fingers and toes.

DIGESTION PROBLEMS. When you slouch, your internal organs are compressed, and this can affect how they function. In the short term, it can lead to constipation, but longer-term, poor posture can negatively and permanently alter your metabolism.[23]

FATIGUE. The body's natural posture is one that takes the least amount of energy to maintain an upright position. Bad posture places strain on parts of you that are not meant to endure it, forcing the body to do extra work and leaving you feeling tired and worn out in the process.

My first awakening to the power of embodiment came through contact with the great Polish theatre director Jerzy Grotowski. He pioneered an approach to acting in which the performer worked to open and free his body so fully that every inner impulse, emotion, thought or image was instantly experienced and visible throughout his body, as it is in a child. This was a radical and powerful idea in theatre, and his work was revered worldwide.

I went to Poland in 1977, by which time Grotowski had stopped directing theatre and was conducting pure research into human potential. A small group of us spent time in a forest outside Wroclaw, where we were led through wild, experimental work. We spent many hours out in nature. We spoke only essential practical information, but we would walk and run together, day and night, with hardly any sleep. It was a freezing winter, yet we were not allowed to wear any protective clothing such as coats or gloves. Amid the hardship and difficulty, there were unforgettable periods of intense physical aliveness and connectedness. I experienced total oneness with the land and the trees, and I still carry these visceral memories.

I subsequently trained in his approach for three years with a sister theatre company in Switzerland,

and then brought the work back to the UK, working as a director and teacher for more than 20 years. The level of embodiment at the work's core was an exciting revelation for many actors I taught at The Royal Academy of Dramatic Art and other drama schools.

Over the years I have engaged with yoga, Hawaiian Kahuna bodywork, running, cycling and various martial arts. For the last two years I have been doing the ancient practice of Qigong for 45 minutes, early most mornings. This keeps me deeply embodied throughout the day, and it opens and stabilizes my body's subtle sensing capacities.

THE PRACTICE

It should be no surprise, then, that conscious, engaged physical activity is a key to restoring connection with the body and maintaining good health. High-performing people often have a strong commitment to exercise and almost all say they do their best thinking, or have their best ideas, when engaged in physical activity. The Leader as Healer embraces physical activity as part of a holistic approach and undertakes regular stretching and exercise to reconnect them to the body. As Arnold Schwarzenegger once said, "A muscle stretched with awareness is 100 times more valuable than mechanical exercise."

This does not mean that you have to take up running, start pumping iron in the gym or become a triathlete, all while leading a complex organization in an ambiguous world. There are many ways you can restore embodiment, and even the smallest commitment – providing it remains consistent at around 3–4 times per week

– will yield transformational results. Even the simple experience of walking in nature with sustained attention can bring you, quite literally, back to your senses.

Conscious breathing can also bring you home to yourself. Think back on the exercise in Chapter One, in which you simply paid attention to your breathing. Perhaps you found that your breath was at first shallow and focused in the chest, and then moved deeper with each inhalation and exhalation, expanding and contracting the stomach. Such a simple exercise can bring you back into the body and enhance clarity and grounding. And this can become a deeply transformative practice that alters everything, moment to moment, throughout your day. In the words of comparative religion and mythology professor Joseph Campbell, in *The Power of Myth*: "People say that what we are seeking is a meaning for life. I think that what we're really seeking is an experience of being alive, so that our experiences on the purely physical plane will have resonance within our innermost being and reality, so that we can actually feel the rapture of being alive."[24]

Through many of the Eastern body-mind disciplines – such as yoga or the martial arts – we learn that the breath carries a vital charge, referred to as *chi*, *qi*, or *prana*. We see this reflected in the terms 'Tai chi' and 'Qigong.' These ancient disciplines consider the nourishment that is provided by the breath of even greater importance to health and longevity than what is found in food and water.

AN EXPERIMENT:

Once you have anchored the difference between thinking and paying attention, see if you can go through your day and, as frequently as possible, bring simple inner awareness to your breathing, just as it is. Notice when it is reduced or contracted and use the outbreath to gently release and soften your body.

As you do this, you will gradually develop the transformational capacity of simultaneous inner and outer attention.

At first, it may seem difficult, but as you relax into the practice you will find, as so many have before you, how much deeper and wider your awareness – of self, others, and your physical surroundings – becomes.

Interestingly, Western science recognizes the importance of negative ions, molecules in the air that carry a negative electrical charge and have a positive impact on human health. Negative ions are most abundant in nature: especially near waterfalls, on mountaintops and in forests, near the ocean, and just after storms. We experience ionized air as invigorating, uplifting and energizing.

In fact, there is evidence that negative ions help neutralize free radicals, enhance cellular metabolism and immune function, and aid in sleep and digestion.[25] Deep breathing increases the number of negative ions brought into the body through the lungs, and thus exerts a powerful therapeutic effect on cells and tissues, helping us to detoxify and recharge.

The following questions are designed to help you reflect on your relationship to embodiment, and how you may work with the topic.

REFLECTION EXERCISE

What is your relationship to your body?

- How much of the time do you feel really connected to your body?
- How much of the time do you live in your body?

In your childhood and adolescence, when were you most connected to your body?

- How was this supported or not?
- To what degree was physical activity embraced by your family? How much hugging and physical contact did you experience from your family?

ACTION

Take your answer to the last question in the reflection exercise and see whether you can create time to do more of it.

Seek out classes and activities that really give you a good feeling in your body. This could be anything from dance, yoga, Qigong, martial arts, going to the gym, cycling or walking.

Commit to one or more of these activities at least four times a week. Even if difficult at first, you should soon find that you enjoy it (and do not want to miss the experience) because of the energy and connectedness it helps you bring forwards into your day.

Above all, whatever form of activity you undertake, connect more consciously with your body. And if you enjoy running outside, *take the earphones out!* Breathe... feel your body... let your senses bathe in the environment.

MOMENT-TO-MOMENT PRACTICE

Practice paying more attention to your physicality throughout the day:

- Notice your breathing as often as you can. Does it feel free or constricted? Where does the breath move?

- Develop the habit of discreetly breathing out more deeply every so often. The outbreath is how you constrict your breathing. Let it go.

- As you walk around, really feel your feet on ground. Try to notice how the pressure rolls along each foot as you walk. Is the ground hard or soft?

- When you are sitting at a computer, pay attention to your breathing and your posture. Where is your breath? Are you slouching? If so, carefully correct your posture as you check in.

CHAPTER 4

A LIFE OF PURPOSE

Many of the leaders with whom I work describe either having lost touch with a sense of purpose or feeling less inspired by their work than before, and they are suffering as a result. Restoration of purpose can have profound, if sometimes unexpected, transformational impacts. Take, for example, the experience of a senior civil servant at one of the largest government departments in the UK. Although he had attained a high level in the government – number two in one of the larger departments – he had applied for the number one position three times but had not been selected.

This senior civil servant came to me to be 'fixed,' so that he finally could be successful. What happened instead was surprising. Rather than focus on his leadership competencies or behaviours, we started by exploring his sense of purpose. After a few meetings, he arrived to our work excited.

"I had a light bulb moment last week," he said. "I realized that I don't really want the job. I was going for it because *that's what you do*. It's the ladder you climb because it's there, and we are told that having the ambition to ascend the ladder is the normal impulse. I've come to realize that there are other paths, and different ways of contributing that are far closer to my heart. And that I can make a much better contribution simply by being true to myself."

THE PRINCIPLE

Living a life without purpose is like navigating a stormy sea with no rudder, anchor or compass. Purpose is essential. As the eminent psychoanalyst Carl Jung reminded us, living without purpose is one of the most grievous wounds of all to the soul.

Purpose has become a hot topic in both personal and professional domains. Individuals can now attend weekend retreats to discover their *raison d'être* – a dubious reflection of our 'quick fix' culture – while on a more serious note, many organizations now seek out the assistance of consultants who can help them define and articulate their core mission, values and purpose.

For some time, the research has shown that many Millennials will willingly join a company whose values they believe in, even if they earn less money.[26] And, like many ideas that are ahead of their time, the concept of

Living a life without purpose is like navigating a stormy sea with no rudder, anchor or compass. Carl Jung reminded us that living without purpose is one of the most grievous wounds of all to the soul.

a 'triple bottom line' – reflecting the value of people, profit, and planet – has now become mainstream.[27] Social media has made it increasingly difficult for organizations to fake this by engaging in what has become known as 'greenwashing' – making bold declarations of social and ecological responsibility that are not genuinely matched by concrete actions.

Although we have yet to digest the deeper lessons of the COVID-19 pandemic, certain phenomena stand out. At the local level, we have seen an outpouring of examples of people showing care and offering mutual support, far beyond the previous 'normal.' And many organizations have come forwards and offered their capacities to help create medical and other essential items, diverting and often significantly reducing their profit streams.

In the mid-2000s, I had a number of conversations with directors of a major business school about the work we were doing with one of the world's biggest defence companies. We discussed how it made sense, socially, morally and fiscally, for the defence contractor to start thinking about how to use their incredible technology for purposes other than war. It has taken a pandemic crisis for this to occur.

The domination of the rational mind and the absence of heart has caused us, too often, to associate a sense of purpose with endless growth, higher productivity and material gain. We have found ourselves perpetually looking for the next thing: the promotion, salary raise, bigger homes, new cars and so on. Yet, what is more soul-destroying than devoting 40–80 hours per week to a job whose purpose does not stretch beyond hitting the next quarter's numbers? Committing yourself to an organization whose 'vision statement' is composed of numbers and targets, rather than values and contribution?

I once saw an advert in a US phone store window which perfectly captures the cycle in which we have trapped ourselves: 'The MORE Everything Plan – Sign up TODAY!'

We want more and more, even without knowing what the *more* we want is. So, we just get more of everything in the hope that it will bring satisfaction. Yet, no amount of money or other material gain comes close to

Purpose arises from the deepest essence of who we are.

the satisfaction we feel simply by living with an imbued sense of purpose and meaning, and with the knowledge that we are making a contribution, be that to one person or ten thousand.

Purpose arises from the deepest essence of who we are, and in a culture of absence we too easily lose touch with that essence. We keep moving, going as fast as possible and working crazy hours to avoid the gnawing sense of emptiness. This works only for a while because, as the American writer Studs Terkel observed: "Work is about a search for daily meaning as well as daily bread, for recognition as well as cash, for astonishment rather than boredom; in short, for a sort of life rather than a Monday-through-Friday sort of dying."[28]

Many of the senior leaders I work with are either at, or coming to, a point of deep reckoning – a sincere and sober questioning of what the point of their lives really is. This often creates a disquieting sense of emptiness, not the spacious feeling of connection that mindfulness brings. There is a dark, cavernous recognition that something is missing, and that there has to be more to life.

We have all been there. I remember one senior executive's remarks from a leadership programme I was running in the US. During a morning break, I found him standing outside amidst a beautiful, snow-covered winter landscape. After a deep session on purpose, he was in a state of shock. He turned to me and quietly said, "This is deep shit." Indeed. But surely better to ask oneself difficult questions about aspiration, meaning and reason now rather than face painful regret in later years.

To find answers to these questions, we need to connect deeply with our heart and body and offer ourselves the space and permission to feel our emotions, whatever they may be. We have to take time, as much as we need, to 'walk around the lake' – time to digest the magnitude of these questions in relation to our own life.

Modern culture often seems ill equipped to help answer such questions. We easily deflect our discomfort, we joke about a 'mid-life crisis,' using humour to avoid feeling our fear and anxiety. Or we buy more stuff. Or we seek to acquire greater status. Or we medicate ourselves in numerous ways, numbing the feeling that all is not well.

Yet, choosing to navigate these questions more consciously often creates a watershed moment, one that heralds deep transformation: the start of a richer, more fulfilled life.

About fifteen years ago, I co-directed Olivier Mythodrama, a successful leadership consultancy that I had helped found.

While in that role, I flew all over the world to work with top teams. First-class flights and five-star hotels became the norm, and I was earning more than I ever imagined possible. But, something had gradually begun to gnaw at my conscience, initially in a nearly inaudible whisper.

It took a carefully guided vision retreat in the Sinai desert to wake me up. A small group of us spent four days preparing for three days of solitude and fasting, during which we would have only water and very basic bedding, laid down in an isolated place, far from anyone.

During those three days, it became clear to me how much I had been seduced by the trappings of the job and the degree to which I had lost sight of my deeper values and purpose. I experienced a painful, yet deeply welcome clarity, and it marked a critical turning point in my life.

It takes courage, and the right timing, to face up to the fact that *more* is not the answer, and that many of the well-polished tools that have led us to success may now need to be respectfully laid down. And, if we are listening, we will sometimes be called to do just that, even without knowing what our new direction will be. At such times, we have to lean into the darkness, rather than run from it, and trust that we will emerge, in a timing not set by us, with a new alignment and a renewed sense of purpose.

One of the most famous lines in world literature speaks directly to this, from Dante's *Inferno*, Canto 1:

> *In the middle of the journey of life*
> *I found myself astray in a dark wood*
> *where the straight road ahead was lost.*

Dante's words echo throughout many traditions, and a century later were captured by Spanish mystic Saint John of the Cross when he described a 'dark night of the soul.' Their mythic nature reveals the universality of personal moments of lostness, which, while deeply challenging, are essential to the journey of life. Though frightening and difficult, they are inflection points for transformation. The ego has gotten us so far, and brought many good things, but now must be gently put aside. Jung perfectly articulated this period as a time for turning inwards, towards 'soul needs' and 'matters of the spirit.'

- What is my true gift to life, my innate contribution?
- To what am I most truly devoted?
- What do I stand for and against?
- How much am I still driven by 'fitting in'?
- Where is the place for wonder, for the sacred or transcendent in my life?
- Can I surrender? Can I bow to something that is greater than myself?

Even if we reject the trappings of traditional religion or other outmoded belief systems (often, for very good reasons), we need not throw away a sense of enchantment. Doing so may leave us estranged from the deeper nature of our experiences, bereft of connection and belonging, alienated from others and from the world. As Einstein noted: "The most beautiful thing we can experience is the mysterious. It is the source of all true art and all science. He to whom this emotion is a stranger, who can no longer pause to wonder and stand rapt in awe, is as good as dead: his eyes are closed."

When we find ourselves in a time of enquiry into the landscape of purpose and transformation, new questions arise:

- What is my true gift to life, my innate contribution?
- To what am I most truly devoted?
- What do I really stand for and against?
- How do I welcome and navigate the sense of unknowing?
- Where are the places of wonder in my life?
- What happens when I open up to what I have always excluded?
- Where is there a place for the sacred or transcendent in my life?
- Can I surrender? Can I bow to something that is greater than myself?

The great Anglo-Irish playwright and polemicist George Bernard Shaw wrote: "This is the true joy in life, being used for a purpose recognized by yourself as a mighty one. Being a force of nature instead of a feverish, selfish little clod of ailments and grievances, complaining that the world will not devote itself to making you happy. I am of the opinion that my life belongs to the whole community and, as long as I live, it is my privilege to do for it what I can. I want to be thoroughly used up when I die, for the harder I work, the more I live. I rejoice in life for its own sake. Life is no brief candle to me. It is a sort of splendid torch which I have got hold of for the moment and I want to make it burn as brightly as possible before handing it on to future generations."

How can we make space for such reflections? We will not find them in business schools, and rarely in books about personal wellbeing and mindfulness. Nevertheless, there is a point at which they can no longer go unanswered, not if we desire lives of meaning and contribution.

Moreover, we cannot create forward-thinking organizations without asking these questions. All over the world, the corporate status quo has been to seek profit at the expense of civilizational survival. It is time to place 'people, profit and planet' at the apex of our work, as the only way in which we create healthy and mutually beneficial profit and contribute to our long-term thriving as a species.

For deeply inspiring examples of large companies that are already fully committed to that path, I highly recommend the work of the academic and 'conscious capitalism' proponent Raj Sisodia.[29]

RECONNECTING TO PURPOSE

The Leader as Healer understands that purpose is lifeblood. And they are willing to ask two central questions:

> *What is the work that is mine to do?*
> *What is it that is being asked of me?*

Take a moment to digest these questions. Accept that there are no quick answers. Instead, allow your asking to invoke a contemplative process, one to live into over many years.

In the work to reconnect the body, mind and heart, the Leader as Healer is one who has developed a strong self-sense, a grounded presence, and a willingness to lean into what he or she stands for and against. The Leader as Healer learns to engage with emotions; to sit with them in openness and receptivity for as long as required. This self-knowing is essential for questions of purpose, and the lack of it may cost us dearly.

In contrast to the rampant self-interest underlying so many of our contemporary crises, the Leader as Healer knows that purpose is born of contribution and service. If this sounds like so much over-idealistic altruism to you, consider that in 2018 psychologists from the University of Chicago's Booth School of Business and Northwestern University's Kellogg School of Management published research showing that the happiness we experience by giving to others lasts much longer than the satisfaction we experience by giving to ourselves. Furthermore, the researchers found that, beyond a certain level of material wellbeing and affluence, having more money *does not* make us happier. In fact, it tends to do the very opposite. This research has since become a pillar among psychological studies into happiness.[30]

The Leader as Healer benefits their teams by asking colleagues:

- What aspects of our work are you proud of?
- What is meaningful to you in the work we are doing together?
- What would you want to tell your grandchildren about our work?

In my experience, most people love an opportunity to reflect and share in this way; it is bonding and energizing. It helps individuals explore their own sense of purpose, and can unlock new feelings of inspiration, clarity, alignment and commitment. Even a realization that we lack purpose can come as a relief when met without judgement.

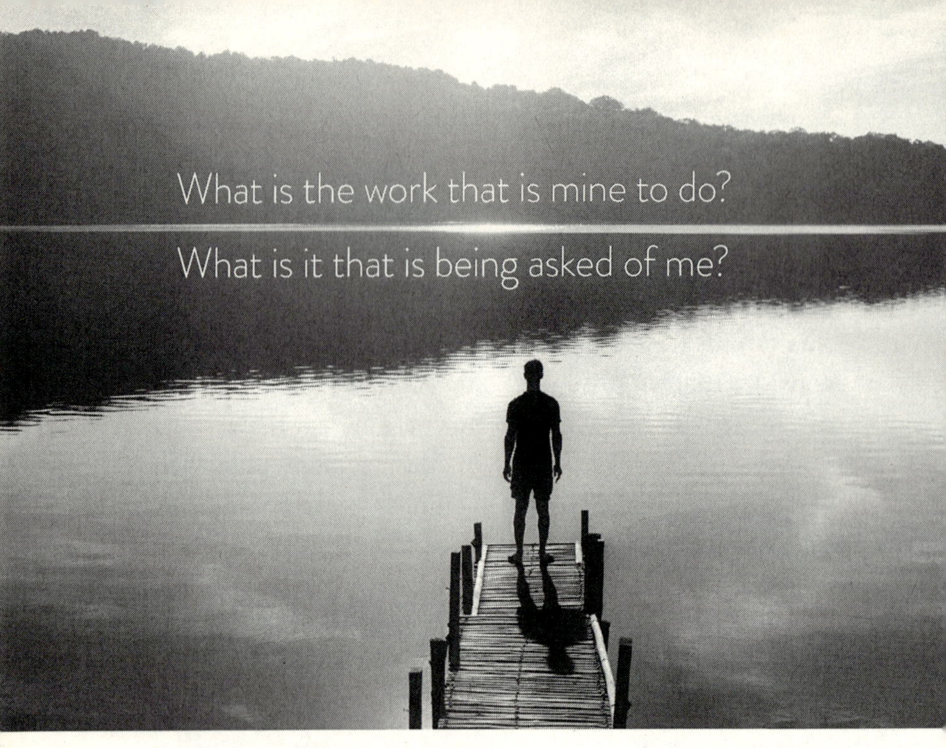

REFLECTION OF A CHIEF EXECUTIVE CLIENT:

Before you can lead an organization towards a purposed vision, you've got to dig deep and find out what your purpose is, what contribution you want to make.

When climbing the corporate ladder is no longer a motivator, then what is it that sustains you? What is it that really drives you?

What do I want to leave in the world for my great-great-grandchildren? And the opportunity to do that as a leader is an incredible privilege.

Below is a simple enquiry, which I encourage everyone to visit regularly:

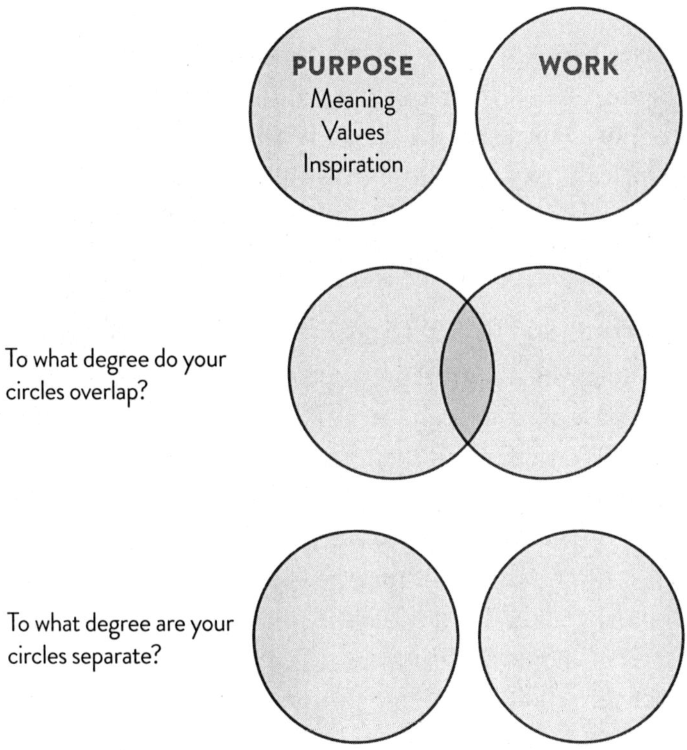

Leaders as Healers are alert to the status of their circles, and will almost certainly experience some periods when they separate. When this happens, we can ask ourselves: Is this a *test* or a *sign*? If it is the former, we will need to re-*vision* something about ourselves or our work, to re-establish the connection. If we conclude it is the latter, it may be time for more radical change, such as leaving our current job or organization.

Generally speaking, there are three ways in which we wake up to and 'recover' from a loss of purpose:

THROUGH A CRISIS, such as severe illness, bereavement, divorce, employment redundancy, etc. A wake-up is not guaranteed by crisis, but there are hundreds of stories of people whose lives were turned upside down by such events, yet emerged with a renewed sense of purpose and direction.[31]

SPONTANEOUS REALIZATION occurs through a moment of recognition, when we realize that our guiding purpose has been lost and must be found. This happened to one of my clients after he treated himself to a walking holiday in the Himalayas in celebration of his 40th birthday. One day, as he sat alone, facing a magnificent mountain panorama, he experienced a sudden recognition of how out of balance his incredibly 'successful' life actually was. This kind of moment usually inspires new life choices and transformational change.

VIA DIALOGUE WITH A MENTOR/COACH. When we find ourselves at a crucial crossroads, we may seek out a companion or coach – a guide with depth and experience. A mentor or coach can encourage us to lean into the unknown and surrender to the darkness, rather than try to get out of it as quickly as possible. Such times often prove to be the most transformational of all.

Indeed, facing questions about the core purpose of our lives needs to be done in a careful, well-supported context.

The first requirement is to create a strong enough space – with the help of a mentor or coach, or in the company of a group of trusted and dedicated friends or colleagues – in which the full spectrum of what is happening can be acknowledged and felt. This is important; we need to keep at bay the impulsive leap to rationalize or fix the experience, even if sitting with it is uncomfortable.

Once we engage wholeheartedly, we often discover two types of tension emerging, both of which need to be welcomed and precisely discerned. The first is the *pull of the past.* As noted previously, the experiences from our early lives that we tried to pack away begin to call for attention and take us to the places within where our fundamental needs – to be received, nurtured, and to belong – were not adequately met. If we allow these places in us to be felt, we begin to see how aspects of the individuals we have become (the 'somebody' we have each attempted to build) were in fact subtly but essentially based in the exclusion of these painful parts of our past. This work requires from us a deep level of vulnerability, but it allows our hearts to melt so that qualities of compassion, connectedness and humility may flourish.

The second tension is the *pull of higher levels of consciousness,* which are simply the successive stages of our human psychological and personal development. If mindfulness brings us to a first level of enhanced spaciousness, here we are called to an entirely different level of consciousness. Art, nature and silence become more essential, and a need for rational certainties recedes further into the background. In traditional cultures, people readily recognized this calling and retired into the forests, deserts or caves, literally or metaphorically, for a period of contemplation. No time limit was set for this task because the need to be in control no longer took precedence. (We will address this more fully in the next chapter.)

The Leader as Healer is committed to creating a culture in which time for deep contemplation can be honoured without having to leave the world. They also embody the kind of leadership and organization that emerges when our tidy, individualistic identities become less rigid, and we are able to embrace a larger field of connectedness, a deeper sense of purpose and a natural instinct for stewardship and service.

THE PRACTICE

The idea of purpose is archetypally associated with the element of fire, which embodies passion, will and action. A Leader as Healer considers those the times in life when they felt most 'on fire.' This is not necessarily a loud or dramatic sensation; it is more a feeling of being intensely aligned with oneself and one's work.

It is also valuable to look back on how and where we have deviated from that sense of alignment. What subtle untruths do we tell ourselves, or others, simply to fit in? In what ways have we compromised our values, and how can we correct this?

REFLECTION EXERCISE

Look back at the times in your life when you felt most aligned with your purpose.

These may be one-off experiences, or they may have lasted months, but on recalling them, contemplate:

- What was happening?
- How did you feel?
  - Try to identify specific emotions and be as precise as possible.

If you were with others, what was the quality of your relationships?

- Did you feel close? Were you well attuned?
- Which core values were you embodying?
- What kind of contribution were you making?
- What parts of your unique abilities and gifts were in play?

Explore several such periods and think/feel into their unifying points.

- How far or close are you to this kind of alignment now?
- In considering that distance, what has caused you to lose touch with the feeling of alignment?
- How might you be compromising or diluting your calling, still driven by a need to 'fit in,' be liked and accepted? To what degree do you still 'play small'?
- What do wish your legacy to be? How do you wish to be remembered?

PRACTICE

Find the places and the activities that allow you to enter a more reflective modality.

Ask yourself:

- To what am I really devoted?
- What breaks my heart?
- What do I love?
- What are my unique gifts and skills?

Let your answers help you to decipher your core values, and identify where you find passion and purpose.

- Read material that inspires you, including biographies, and spend time with music or other art forms that touch you deeply.
- Start a journal of reflection. At the end of each day, write down what has touched you, what surprised you and which moments or interactions felt fresh and alive.

- Speak with close friends and colleagues about purpose, values, inspiration and meaning.
- Try writing poems or free-flowing text about what most touches or inspires you. These do not need to be long or perfectly written – no one else need ever see them. Just write about your passions.

On a hot day in Egypt in 1982, I made the long climb upwards to the main chamber of the Great Pyramid of Giza. Inside, there were only the stark, stone walls and a solitary open stone sarcophagus. As soon as I arrived in the chamber, I was transfixed by the atmosphere. After a few minutes, I found myself immersed in an altered state, similar to those I had experienced during meditative and creative practices, except for its unusual intensity. I closed my eyes and soon lost all sense of time. I felt as if I were standing in the epicentre of a great energy vortex.

Eventually, a small group of other tourists arrived, and it was clear that they were irritated by the climb. Within seconds of arriving, a woman angrily proclaimed, "There's nothing here!" and stormed out, followed quickly by her companions.

In contemporary culture, we have lost the terrain in which the transpersonal is transparent. So it indeed seems that 'nothing is here.' As a result, we are often truly lost.

CHAPTER 5

MINDFULNESS AND MEDITATION

THE PRINCIPLE

Meditation and mindfulness are two of the most important and powerful resources of the Leader as Healer. Both practices help to open and stabilize the inner dimension of *being*, ensuring that we operate with the widest bandwidth possible and are able to draw on all our faculties. The essential foundation provided by the contemplative practices helps us to access a quality of deep inner stillness, even amidst the noise and mayhem that so often surrounds us, whether in complex business environments, amid divisive politics, during a global pandemic or in a time of accelerating climate change.

As more and more leaders are discovering, such practices are crucial. They offer a vital lifeline in a volatile world by aiding our ability to take a broader perspective, rather than getting trapped in the tunnel vision of an immediate situation. The world's turbulence will not disappear, but when we are able to access the stillness within, we no longer need it to. We learn to operate from a place of great inner depth so that even when we find ourselves buffeted by the headwinds, our ballast never fails us.

Under the domination of the rational mind, we become trapped in a dimension of reality that rests solely on what we can see in front of us. But by dedicating ourselves to meditation and mindfulness practices, we can begin to access deeper levels of *beingness* and a new quality of inner silence. And we discover that there is no end to the depth and gift of that silence.

The new levels of awareness that such practices activate have been described throughout history and across cultures, and are thoroughly researched by contemporary science. Over the last 3,000 years, small groups of people in every culture have explored the nature of human consciousness and discovered means by which to develop and expand it. Many such groups formed an esoteric core within their culture's established religion, and often chose to live in monasteries, ashrams or remote wilderness locations, apart from the everyday world. Regardless of culture or religion, their explorations – and the universal truths they uncovered – became central to what we now refer to as the world's great wisdom traditions.

Some of these spiritual communities were accepted and respected, while others were rejected or even persecuted and exiled, particularly in times when orthodox religion stood as the centremost agent of power and control in a given society. Other groups hid or withheld their teachings in the belief that, if people were not properly prepared or initiated, learning the teachings could be counterproductive or even destructive.

From the ancient Mayans and early Kabbalists to the great yogi masters of India and Native American shamans, many of the old traditions foresaw our current era of volatility, uncertainty and incredible change with impressive accuracy. They predicted that this period would be a time when their teachings would be most needed and should, therefore, be made available.

We see their foresight reflected in the widespread surge of interest in the practice of mindfulness, now used in schools, hospitals, prisons and many organizations worldwide. The benefits for some inner-city schools with high incidents of violence are remarkable and well documented, and in many forward-thinking organizations the practice of mindfulness has become part of the daily calendar.

Countless high-profile CEOs and public figures have said publicly that meditation is an essential part of their lives, including Jeff Weiner, Ariana Huffington, Russell Simmons, Joe Rogan, Bob Shapiro, Padmasree Warrior, Andrew Chert, Marc Benioff, Oprah Winfrey, Bob Stiller, Bill Gates, Bill George, Ramani Ayer, Steve Rubin, David Lynch and Jerry Seinfeld. Ray Dalio, founder of the world's largest hedge fund, said: "Meditation has probably been the single most important reason for whatever success I've had."

The new levels of awareness
that meditation practices activate
have been described throughout
history and across cultures, and
are thoroughly researched by
contemporary science.

CLIENT MEMO: SHARED WITH ME BY A SENIOR VICE PRESIDENT FROM A MULTI-NATIONAL TECHNOLOGY CORPORATION

"Since you worked with us, we now start all important meetings with five minutes of silence, eyes closed. At first, it felt slightly awkward but very quickly became essential, because the results are so clear.

"Since we agreed to take this short time to settle, to connect with ourselves and to the presence of the group, the quality of our thinking, as well as our sense of mutual connectedness, has dramatically transformed.

"Fascinating to realize that, one year ago, it would have been unthinkable to do this."

Even if modern mindfulness practice is a watered-down version of its source teaching, the upsurge of interest seems to represent a crucial correction to the separation and disconnection we discussed in earlier chapters. It is as if humanity subconsciously understands just how urgently this correction is needed. And, it is no accident that the practice of mindfulness usually begins with an invitation to bring more awareness to our bodies, thus opening the gateways described in Chapter 2.

There are many known benefits of mindfulness practice, including:

- Stress reduction
- Improved wellbeing and resilience
- Better quality of relationships
- Heightened capacity to focus
- Improved decision-making
- Increased skill for collaboration

Valuable as these benefits are, most still belong to the 'me' domain and are all about improving how *I* function. In our self-obsessed culture, it is easy to forget the deeper purpose of mindfulness and meditation: to dissolve the experience of separation; to broaden and transform one's sense of I/me; and to open oneself to the mystery of a deeply unified field.

There are, perhaps, no better words to capture this mystery than Einstein's: "A human being is part of a whole called by us 'Universe,' a part limited in time and space. He experiences himself, his thoughts and his feelings as something separated from the rest, a kind of optical delusion of his consciousness. This delusion is a ... prison for us, restricting us to our personal desires and to affection for a few persons nearest to us. Our task must be to free ourselves from this prison by widening our circle of compassion to embrace all living creatures and the whole of nature in its beauty."

Einstein was touching on what psychology calls the *transpersonal*, or the transcendent. We might also call it 'inner silence' or 'spaciousness,' or whatever feels right. As we experience these domains, we discover a dimension of reality far beyond the ordinary world of the here and now. The transpersonal realm is entirely different from and unaffected by the events of 2022. Put simply: it always was, always is, and always will be. Nothing can ever change that. Connecting into and stabilizing this dimension in our awareness allows us to navigate the here-and-now world in an entirely different way.

It has been experienced and described in every culture since time immemorial.

Meditation and mindfulness break our limited fixation on just the 'black letters,' and open our capacities of perception to take in whole new dimensions of consciousness – the 'white page' and beyond.

Dee Hock, the founder of Visa International, once wrote: "What if the very concept of separability is a grand delusion of Western civilization, epitomized by the Industrial Age, useful in certain scientific ways of knowing, but fundamentally flawed with respect to understanding and wisdom? What if our notions of separability, particularity, and measurement are just a momentary aberration in the great evolution of consciousness?"[32]

The core teachings of the world's wisdom traditions converge around a central theme of awakening: a profound feeling of 'waking up' to a new quality of awareness that shakes us out of the culture of absence, as if we are waking from a dream.

Through our work together, hundreds of leaders have been able to deepen an existing meditation practice or begin a new one. All report experiencing significant benefit, even if they initially found practice difficult.

Often, the result is a greater sense of ease and effectiveness. Many clients tell me they now get more done in less time, and experience more energy and less fatigue.

For others, a more profound opening occurs. A sense of inner silence grows stronger, enabling them to perceive self, other and the world in a more multi-layered, multi-faceted way. They discover a new orientation to 'soul values' and a deeper experience of purpose. As this unfolds, previous habitual drives and desires diminish in influence, and are replaced with a feeling of connectedness and presence, in life and work.

Many of these leaders, like the executive quoted a few pages earlier, have introduced a group practice: just a few minutes of silence taken by all at the start of meetings.

The core teachings of the world's wisdom traditions converge around a central theme of awakening: a profound feeling of 'waking up' to a new quality of awareness that shakes us out of the culture of absence, as if we are waking from a dream. In place of absence, there is now presence: *I am here, and I am available.* We are at once sophisticated rational thinkers, emotional feelers, intuitive knowers, imaginative creators and embodied physical forms. All aspects of the self are engaged in a continual state of flow, and simultaneously rooted in an unchangeable stillness or silence. Our ability to rest in *beingness* deepens, however busy and active our *doingness* becomes. Our practice of the 'backward circle' naturally deepens and opens us to new dimensions.

The wisdom traditions all speak in some form of:

- A move from separateness into an experience of connection and unity – an awareness of the interdependence of everything
- The ability to access a core level of inner stillness, spaciousness and an emptiness that is paradoxically filled with a magnificent immanence (distinct from the arid emptiness that is a hallmark of depression)
- Greater self-sufficiency or satisfaction from the inside and, therefore, less dependence on objects, status, praise, recognition or validation to fulfil us
- A transformation in thinking: from scarcity consciousness to abundance consciousness

- The awakening of deep compassion and an innate drive towards altruism
- Reduced attachment to the personal ego

The wisdom traditions also emphasize *attention* as the single greatest tool we have for transforming consciousness. Ordinarily, our attention is directed by the rational mind and bound by what we can perceive with the five senses. (Remember the disappointed woman I encountered inside the Great Pyramid?) Yet, the traditions teach that what we agree to call 'reality,' however compelling it may be, is in fact an infinitesimal piece of the greater whole. Indeed, what we pay attention to shapes our reality, so by changing how and to what we pay attention, we expand both ourselves and our world.

We are just beginning to witness a rich and very significant marriage between the hard facts of contemporary science and the deeper insights of the world's ancient core traditions. Neuroscience research has been able to show that brain activity is changed by the practice of mindfulness, which impacts everything from brainwave frequency to function to brain matter volume. For example, when a subject practices paying attention more consciously, their brainwave frequency moves from the beta range (from 14 to 20Hz) observed in normal waking consciousness, to alpha waves (from 8 to 13Hz) observed during daydreaming, meditation and the experience of flow states, such as those experienced by athletes when 'in the zone.' Many artists, writers and scientists report their own moments of flow during which they experience heightened creativity, deep insights and seemingly effortless productivity.

Consider the words of psychologist Frances Vaughan: "Time after time it appears that major human achievements involve intuitive leaps of imagination. It is the intuitive, holistic, pattern-perception faculties associated with the right hemisphere of the brain that break through existing formulations of truth and expand the body of knowledge. The stabilization of intuitive insights, and their usefulness to humanity, are subsequently determined by careful, logical examination and validation, but the original vision or insight is intuitive."[33]

Legendary rock musician Carlos Santana put it this way: "As Miles Davis would say, 'You just shut up.' Tell your mind to shut up. Turn off the TV, turn off the radio, and you start hearing this blend of voices – angels, demons – and, all of a sudden, they become one note, one voice, one melody, and you grab it. Most of the time it comes from when you're deeply still; that's the best music that comes."[34]

Meditation and mindfulness help loosen our fixation with the world of black letters and create an opening through which we recognize the white page, or new dimensions of consciousness.

This provides us with a rich new set of tools. With them, we discover the capacity to:

- Relocate and reside in a deep level of 'being,' from which we operate with much greater clarity and steadiness, even in the midst of a volatile world
- Perceive circumstances and events with much greater context and understanding – with expanded consciousness – allowing us to see far more than the black and white world in front of us and into rich layers of nuance, subtle signals and the whispers of a more holistic intelligence
- Operate as a coherent whole, from mind, body and heart, enabling us to:
  - › Attune more deeply to situations and respond wisely, rather than letting our habitual, unconscious reactions take over
  - › Bring a higher quality of attention and presence to our relations with others, including colleagues and teams, which activates new levels of potential all around us

Through mindfulness and meditation practices, the Leader as Healer learns to participate in both the black letters and the white page. This fosters a more intimate connection with all aspects of life, including with what we term the transcendent.

In the words of the great 13th-century Persian poet Jalal ad-Din Muhammad Rumi: "Live in the Nowhere that you came from, even though you have an address here."

Be busy. But, find ways to access your essential beingness and remember that you are part of something vast and timeless. The path of the Leader as Healer is a lifelong journey towards mastery. Those who follow it faithfully uncover startling new levels of insight and innovation, and deeper possibilities for all forms of relationship. Along the way, the Leader as Healer learns to make visible the transpersonal, and make increasingly consistent contact with the transcendent.

The 20th-century theoretical physicist David Bohm put it this way: "If you reach deeply into yourself, you are reaching into the very essence of mankind. When you do this, you will be led into the generating depth of consciousness that is common to the whole of mankind and that has the whole of mankind enfolded in it. The individual's ability to be sensitive to that becomes the key to the change of mankind. We are all connected. If this could be taught, and if people could understand it, we would have a different consciousness."[35]

THE PRACTICE

I invite and encourage you to take up mindfulness and meditation practices until they come to effortlessly reside at the centre of your life. As with any new practice, this necessitates intention and commitment. While meditation requires that you take time apart (to begin, set aside 20 minutes to sit quietly), mindfulness can be practiced throughout the day, wherever you are and within whatever you are doing, thus eliminating the 'I don't have time' barrier.

An important note: 'paying attention' has *nothing to do with thinking*. Initially, it is easy to conflate the two, but understanding their distinction is important. Thinking is a left-brain function; *paying attention* is a primary and foundational function.

The core principle of mindfulness is to deliberately and unconditionally pay attention to whatever is arising.

'Deliberately' means choosing over and over how and to what you pay attention, while 'unconditionally' means noticing exactly what is happening inside you – physically, emotionally and mentally – without seeking to analyse or change it.

There are several reasons why this can be difficult at first:

- Our nervous system gets habituated to certain levels of activation, with an accompanying physical chemistry. The act of consciously paying attention is a completely new factor or frequency coming in that initially counters this activation; we are essentially detoxing. This makes regular practice essential: while initially uncomfortable, the detox gradually brings relief and a sense of settling and inner alignment
- The dominance of the rational mind demands that we understand everything, so that we can feel in control. The act of paying attention without condition or analysis challenges this deep-seated impulse. As we gradually relocate ourselves in the experience of beingness, we begin to notice how thinking does *not* have to dominate. Over time, the energy required to feel in control lessens, and we may experience a huge sense of relief and internal relaxation. This impulse is slowly replaced by an openness to subtle sensing and insights that we previously had little space for

- Last, but not least, as our grip on thinking loosens, we begin to experience an expanded sense of awareness. And we may discover new layers of emotion within us. Learning to work appropriately with the emotions is an essential part of our development, as we covered in Chapter 3

With regular practice these difficulties soon ease. By connecting regularly to body, emotion and purpose, we discover a potent path of restoration – of 'coming home' – and the vital insights this path produces become embedded at the core of our lives.

Committed practice has two components:

- Mindfulness, throughout the day
- Daily meditation

PRACTICING MINDFULNESS

Practicing mindfulness throughout the day expands one's bandwidth of perception and deepens the capacity for embodied presence.

- The most concrete and transformative practice is to *learn to pay inner and outer attention at the same time*. As you apply this practice, you will notice how much more present you feel and how much better you listen

- The best way to anchor this practice is by learning to keep some portion of attention in the body at all times – remember the 'back-ward circle'.
  - › Start with your breathing. Pay attention to your breath and, once that is established, include an awareness of the soles of your feet
  - › When you are walking around, sitting at your desk or in a meeting, keep these channels of inner awareness open

Because we are breaking long-embedded habits and installing new ones, it is usually essential to find clear ways to remind yourself to practice awareness. Without reminders, it is too easy to forget.

The following reminders have been tried and tested by hundreds of leaders I have worked with:

- Buy a new pen. Whenever you are in a meeting, put the pen on the table so that every time you look at it, you are reminded to focus on your breathing. If it has become tight and constricted, gently expand it by lengthening the outbreath
- Each time your phone rings, let it prompt you to take one deep, conscious breath, feel your feet, and *then* answer the call. Bonus: you will likely notice an incredible improvement in the quality of your calls
- Carry a small object in your pocket, such as a pebble. Touch it regularly as a reminder to focus on embodiment
- Place visual images around your workspace as reminders to notice the body, and to breathe
- Programme your phone to send visual reminders as notifications
- Use one of the excellent apps, such as Headspace, Calm or Waking Up, that have reminder functions built in

CREATING A MEDITATION PRACTICE

Dedicate a time each day to sit quietly, eyes closed, with the spine in a gentle, upright position.

- Try to practice on a regular schedule; early mornings before breakfast are often the best time to practice
- Chose a set location in which to meditate
- Resting in meditation just after a physical workout, however briefly, will almost always be beneficial to the mind and body

Meditation can be done purely by sitting, without guidance or aid, or it can involve attentional exercises and/or audio guidance, which the apps mentioned above can provide. It is important to understand that we are not trying to *stop* thinking. This may happen occasionally, but it is not the goal. The goal is to locate ourselves in the inner space *beyond* our thinking, without too much effort or fixation.

Each sitting will be different. Let go of needing it to be any particular way. Some days your ‘monkey mind’ will chatter incessantly, other days you may feel blissfully peaceful. Through consistent practice know that you are opening new (and measurable) neural pathways in your brain and, over time, the results and benefits will be very clear.

PURE SITTING PRACTICE

Set a timer to alert you after 20 minutes, an hour or whatever period feels best. Then:

- Gently focus your awareness on your breathing. Try to notice every detail of each inbreath and outbreath
- Next, allow yourself to feel the distinct sensations that arise in all parts of your body, including those areas that feel numb or disconnected. Simply notice
- After a while, expand your attention to include any sounds occurring around you. Just hear them – no need to analyse. You will likely notice many sounds you were not previously aware of
- Gradually turn your awareness to the growing sense of inner spaciousness, inner quiet
- Whenever you become distracted by thoughts (a normal occurrence), simply notice it. Then, redirect your awareness back to your breathing and to the quality of inner silence

CHAPTER 6

THE CALL

Approximately 3.5 billion years ago, microscopic single-cell organisms appeared deep in the planet's oceans. More than three million years ago, our evolutionary forebears invented the first tools. It took another two million years before they learned to use fire, and another 80,000, give or take, for our ancestors to begin crafting clay vessels, weave clothing from natural fibres, take up agriculture and invent the wheel.[36] By comparison, modern humans live in a time of exponential technological growth and radical planetary change. In just the last 20 years, we have witnessed the emergence and widespread proliferation of smartphones, Facebook, driverless cars, gene editing, 3D printing and video conferencing, to name just a few developments. Some estimates suggest there has been more technological advance in the last five years than in the previous 500.

Change: it is coming faster and faster. And massive change begets both massive disruption and massive opportunity, if we can adapt.

Humanity's intractable social and systemic problems have propagated just as quickly, such that ecological crisis now poses an existential threat, to us and countless other species. If we are believers in science or readers of history, we take that threat seriously. After all, societies have failed and civilizations collapsed under far less. The difference now is that we are one, inextricably interconnected global civilization.

What is it that leaders most need to understand, and hopefully become, in order to generate truly adaptive strategies at the evolutionary edge?

As Otto Scharmer, senior lecturer at MIT and bestselling author, writes: "This is the moment when what we need most is enough people with the skill, heart and wisdom to help us pull ourselves back from the edge of breakdown and onto a different path."[37]

While enormous amounts of power are wielded by the few, many still struggle just to get by. The work of governments and institutions worldwide is often dominated by self-interest, and the artefacts of global culture reflect the same drives. While quality of life has vastly improved in many parts of the world, the globalization of bottomless greed, ceaseless competition and hyper-consumption have brought humanity to peril. Economic, political and social inequality is rampant and extreme, driven by different types of self-interest far more than concern for the good of the whole.

Difficult as it may be to face, these drivers are leading us collectively towards the genuine possibility of civilization collapse, partial or total. In the words of theoretical physicist, futurist and bestselling author Michio Kaku: "We still have the same sectarian, fundamentalist, irrational passions of our ancestors, but the difference is that now we have nuclear, chemical and biological weapons.[38] Climate scientists in all parts of the world agree: humanity's impact on the planet has reached a red-alert crisis. For any hope of slowing, much less reversing, the trend, we must look beyond technological and economic growth and seek to advance our shared ethical, moral, emotional and spiritual intelligence.

With news so ominous, how are we to prepare for potential catastrophe, yet simultaneously work together to reduce the worst of it? What outmoded mindsets need to be transcended if we are to thrive, not just survive, in our organizations and societies?

I believe that the gravity of this moment is an unprecedented evolutionary opportunity: the choice to integrate timeless contemplative wisdom with the advances of modern science and psychology.

Throughout this book, I have touched on what may be seen as a root cause of the danger we are in: namely, the degree to which our rational, left-brain function has risen to dominance, resulting in the subjugation of emotional awareness and suppression of our innate sensing capacities. Let us remember that the rational mind can only think and analyse; it does not *feel*. With this, we have lost the foundational experience of *connectedness* – with ourselves, with one another and with the world.

At the organizational level, we have been attempting to manage greater and greater complexity with tools that are no longer fit for purpose. At the societal level, we struggle to address accelerating large-scale challenges and polarizations without access to the deeper levels of insight and wisdom that arise when all parts of us work as a coherent whole.

Yet, we deeply crave the connection that more holistic states would bring.

The gravity of this moment is an unprecedented evolutionary opportunity: the choice to integrate timeless contemplative wisdom with the advances of modern science and psychology.

Sport, for instance, is one of the more popular ways in which we taste this state, and is the reason I devoted so many years to the study of 'the zone.' Consider the words of Bill Russell, the famous Boston Celtics basketball player:

> "Every so often, a Celtics game would heat up so that it became more than a physical or even a mental game and would be magical. That feeling is very difficult to describe, and I certainly never talked about it when I was playing. When it happened, I could feel my play rise to a new level. It came rarely and would last anywhere from five minutes to a whole quarter or more... It would surround not only me and the other Celtics, but also the players on the other team, even the referees. At that special level, all sorts of odd things happened. The game would be in a white heat of competition, and yet, somehow, I wouldn't feel competitive – which is a miracle in itself. I'd be putting out the maximum effort... and yet I never felt the pain. The game would move so fast that everything was surprising and yet nothing could surprise me. It was almost as if we were playing in slow motion. During those spells, I could almost sense how the next play would develop and where the next shot would be taken... My premonitions would be consistently correct, and I always felt then that I not only knew all of the Celtics by heart, but also all the opposing players, and that they all knew me... These were the moments when I had chills pulsing up and down my spine."[39]

To experience that state as a performer, and to be in the presence of such flow as a spectator, is deeply enlivening and inspiring. We often talk about such moments for years afterwards, so that very special sports events come to acquire an almost mythical status in the collective consciousness. Yet, while we endlessly study and devote countless resources to cultivating such 'magical' moments, we don't really know how to situate these experiences within a larger context, and therefore cannot always fully see their implications. In reality, powerful 'in the zone' moments are windows to an expanded and coherent consciousness, one that defies our ordinary experience of separation and disconnection.

Without exception, every leader I have worked with, whether individually or in groups, has experienced moments of 'that feeling.' Such experiences may be rare, or almost forgotten, yet their value is laden with meaning. They momentarily change the way we perceive the world and bring us into higher, more coherent levels of performance. And every leader, indeed, every person I have ever met wishes their lives were more permeated by this sensibility.

It is as if we are collectively caught between two very different stories about reality and what it means to be human and, therefore, what our responsibilities are. One story is that of material determinism: we live in a basically 'dead' universe; our intellectual, moral and cultural choices are determined solely by material factors; what we call 'consciousness' is simply a by-product of the physical brain. This reality is encapsulated in the 'black letters,' and is the standard story of mainstream Western science.

The other story is one of a living universe, in which consciousness is the *prima materia*. As authors like Fritjof Capra, Thomas Berry and many others note, it is a 'new story,' one that emerges in the synthesis of ancient religious wisdom and the data of the scientific leading edge. It is simultaneously there in the black letters *and* the white page.

It is a story that changes everything. And, it places us at a pivotal moment in human evolution.

The leadership we need now does not try to escape the complexity of the world, but rather develops a capacity for effectiveness that acknowledges that the fundamental reality is one of inherent unity. That's why the primary revolution that we need is more a spiritual revolution than a political or economic one, as badly needed as the latter are.

The leadership we need now does not try to escape the complexity of the world, but rather develops a capacity for effectiveness that acknowledges that the fundamental reality is one of inherent unity.

THE RETURN FROM EXILE

Perhaps the most painful suffering we have unwittingly created is the loss of sacredness in our lives, the loss of awe regarding the Mystery in which we are enfolded. I again quote Einstein: "The most beautiful thing we can experience is the mysterious. It is the source of all true art and all science. He to whom this emotion is a stranger, who can no longer pause to wonder and stand rapt in awe, is as good as dead: his eyes are closed. To know that what is impenetrable for us really exists and manifests itself as the highest wisdom and the most radiant beauty, whose gross forms alone are intelligible to our poor faculties – this knowledge, this feeling... that is the core of the true religious sentiment. In this sense, and in this sense alone, I rank myself among profoundly religious men."

I confess that, in exactly that sense, I, too, am and always have been a deeply religious man, looking to find how to live that sensibility in our secular world without becoming entwined with traditional forms and dogma.

In the preceding pages, I have attempted to outline a theoretical and practical path to the kind of evolutionary leadership I believe is now essential across all domains: the personal, organizational and societal. It is a path of *restoration*, through which we strive to reintegrate previously exiled aspects of our nature: physical, emotional and transpersonal. On this pathway, the brilliance and sophistication of the thinking mind takes its rightful place alongside the sensing and feeling mind, together creating a much larger, more holistic intelligence.

Over and over again, in individual senior leaders and their teams, I have seen the evidence: when people finally feel safe enough to *slow down* and experience more personal and interpersonal connectedness, within body, heart and soul, there is an enormous sense of release. There is release from the nightmare of a racing mind, the relentless sense of pressure, the feeling of never having enough time. Finally, there is a profound easing — an inner settling, and a new sense of being.

And it is from that settling that we begin to experience a refinement in critical thinking, access new and higher levels of intelligence, and witness genius, inspiration and insight pouring in.

The most painful suffering we have unwittingly created is the loss of sacredness in our lives, the loss of awe regarding the Mystery in which we are enfolded.

THE CALL

As a theatre director, I frequently observed two distinct types of actor: the technically competent actor and the 'surrendered' actor.

The former might approach me with a dilemma: "I don't know what to do with this speech." My reply was always the same: "Whatever you do with this speech is of small interest compared to what *it* will do with *you*." Throughout 20 years of work with actors, I researched how to help them lean consistently into what it meant to be a 'channel,' a container through which intense frequencies from the full spectrum of humanity could flow, just as they do in any great live musical performance.

When an actor understood this, they were able to speak one line of Shakespeare, for instance, with a completely new impulse of emotion, an unforeseen eruption of energy and aliveness. And, if they had learned how to *surrender* to such flow, to give themselves 'as if in love,'[40] then we, in the theatre or the rehearsal room, could be moved to our very core. I remember instances in which the simple words 'thank you,' spoken at a climactic moment of a Shakespeare play, could reduce almost an entire audience to tears.

Through the surrendered performer, we find ourselves in the presence of magnificent life force. It is no wonder that people were willing to camp on a sidewalk overnight in sub-zero, midwinter New York to get tickets to see an opera artist like Maria Callas, who gave herself so fully to that force.

The great artist, like the great scientist and the great leader, has matured enough to realize that the higher levels of creativity, insight and innovation we crave are not something we do. Rather, they *do us*. They recognize when it is time to step aside, relinquish control and demonstrate a balance between being and doing. The Leader as Healer has matured enough to know how to bow and surrender to the emergence of new ideas and higher insights. They understand first that many of the innovations we currently need will arrive in this way, and secondly that we cannot know what these emergent qualities will be until they appear. Our task is to cultivate the receptivity in us.

Yesterday's leaders were masters of incremental change and gradual shift, and were selected and rewarded for their powers of profit-maximization. Today's leaders must possess potent powers for logic, reason, discernment and strategic forecasting, yet must *also* be empathic and therefore embodied; grounded and therefore intuitive; present and therefore awake. They must be skilled in mindfulness and deep listening; present and receptive to higher levels of insight and innovation; able to inspire authentic engagement and collaboration; and possess a clear and wholehearted sense of service, mission, and purpose. They are called upon to restore coherence where there is fragmentation and unity where there is division.

They must be both intentional and surrendered, able to embrace the volatility, uncertainty, complexity and ambiguity of our time, so as to become agents through which radical disruption transmutes into radical opportunity, and planetary crisis into global transformation.

They are the heralds of a new future.

This is *Leader as Healer.*

Your time is now.

The Leader as Healer has matured enough to know how to bow and surrender to the emergence of new ideas and higher insights.

POSTSCRIPT
NICHOLAS JANNI'S STORY

I was born in London in 1954, the only child of an affluent show business family.

My father, an Italian Jew, had been raised in Milan. He studied engineering at university but was keenly interested in film. He entered one of his films in the Venice Film Festival amateur section and won first prize. But, when they realized that he was Jewish, they refused to award it to him. His response? "One day, I'll return and win the main prize."

Which he did.

As the Second World War approached, the Italian Jewish population suffered increasing restriction and persecution. Seeing what was coming, my grandfather agreed to an operation that he knew he would almost certainly not survive, and my father, grandmother and uncle were forced to flee their home in Italy. To his dismay, my father found himself interned for a time as an 'enemy alien' at Metropole Internment Camp on the Isle of Man.

After the war ended, my father's love of film was reignited, and he went on to became one of the world's top film producers. With his close friend director John Schlesinger, he made *Billy Liar, A Kind of Loving, Darling, Far from the Madding Crowd, Sunday Bloody Sunday* and *Yanks*. And, he made films with other greats: Joseph Losey, Franco Zeffirelli and Ken Loach.

My mother was of Welsh origin, brought up in an upper middle-class family in Brighton, and was one of the first women to earn a scholarship to study at Oxford University. A brilliant, vivacious and exceptionally beautiful woman, she met my father while working as an assistant on one of his early films.

My parents lived a 'celebrity' lifestyle in Chelsea; film stars of the day were our regular house guests. It was the Swinging Sixties and we lived near the famous King's Road (something I was rather proud of). Ours was a high energy, always exciting, but also deeply volatile home, and only later did I understand how thick the air had been with my parent's unspoken, unhealed trauma.

During the war, my mother's only sibling had died in his Supermarine Spitfire, a single-seat fighter plane, his loss made worse by the fact that neither his aircraft nor his body were ever found. My uncle had simply gone out on a mission and never returned. Years later, I learned from a family friend that, at around 19 years old, my mother experienced a nervous breakdown. Though it was never openly discussed, she was eventually diagnosed with manic depression, or what is now termed bipolar illness.

Despite these emotional hardships, she was a tremendously dedicated mother. I remember how she always stood on the touchline during my school football matches, whatever the weather. Still, over time her mental health challenges became increasingly evident.

As for my father, he lived out the rest of his life in the UK, an exile in more ways than one. Like so many other Holocaust survivors, he ploughed onwards by burying not just the trauma, but his entire identity as a Jew, including any relic of religiosity or spirituality. In fact, he became vehemently atheist, which meant that I grew up with almost no references to, and certainly no understanding of that part of who we were.

While my mother's emotional instability grew, matched in intensity by the disabling lows of chronic fatigue, my father regularly erupted with a volcanic rage. At nine years old, I was sent away to boarding school. Initially, I was overwhelmed by the pain of separation, a trauma in its own right and the basis for the UK therapy group Boarding School Survivors. Later, however, I began to love being at school. It was there that I made my first 16mm film and where I had my first powerful theatre experience, playing the role of Lady Macbeth. I still remember our excellent drama teacher and the intensity with which we performed.

At 16, my life radically changed direction.

At school in London, I was fully immersed in the teenage counterculture of the times – sex, drugs and rock and roll – to which academic study became a tedious interference. It was the norm to listen to Pink Floyd, Yes, The Nice and others play live at all-night concerts. But as one school holiday approached, I was invited to accompany a friend on a visit to his grandmother in Scotland. She lived as a nun at Samye Ling, a Tibetan Buddhist monastery near Lockerbie. Although it is now one of the biggest such communities in Europe, Samye Ling was then just one house, founded by the famous Tibetan lama, Chögyam Trungpa.

I spent the first few days there amused and fascinated by the exotic nature of the place: the lavishly decorated meditation hall filled with Tibetan monks performing prayers, prostrations, chants, and seemingly endless meditation. I had never seen anything like it.

One day, someone lent me a classic Buddhist text which I sat down one afternoon to read. It suggested that we each live inside a small, tightly conditioned experience of self and the world, one that conceals something much deeper and vastly more real. Suddenly – I cannot know how or why – it was as if an enormous curtain had been torn open, exposing this truer, vaster reality to me.

I had never thought about such things, yet immediately understood in my bones the truth of what I was reading. It irrevocably altered the course of my life. Ever since, the drive to explore the deeper self and the more expanded sense of reality that ancient text pointed towards has been the central focus of my life.

I had no idea how or where to begin, of course. But, I sat and copied a long piece of Buddhist text – one that made little sense at all to me, then. Once back at school, I persuaded my friend that we should spend evenings reading the words aloud to each other. In a bout of youthful passion and naivety, I wrote a ten-page letter to my parents, attempting to explain what I had experienced. Needless to say, my atheist father didn't take it very well; my letter marked the beginning of a great and regrettable distance between us.

Before long, however, other guiding voices appeared. I was particularly enraptured by philosopher and theologian Alan Watts and his commentaries on Zen Buddhism, and the books of Carlos Castaneda, which purported to describe his studies with an Indian shaman in Mexico. Another friend and I began to explore these topics wholeheartedly, and I became deeply interested in the experience of peak states, or what I came to know as 'flow states.' Together, we formed a dedicated two-person spiritual seeker group. We did yoga and studied classical piano. And, whenever we could, we trekked to the Welsh mountains to ascend a high peak, before running down as fast as we could, hoping to achieve the altered states described by Castaneda, in which 'lines of energy' could be seen.

More or less by default, I chose to study the arts at university. (I was, anyway, spectacularly hopeless in subjects like physics or chemistry.) In the months before starting my drama course, I found myself leafing through books at a second-hand bookshop in Cecil Court, a pedestrian street in London's historic Covent Garden. I'd come to a little-known book, *Towards a Poor Theatre*, by Jerzy Grotowski, the innovative Polish theatre director and theorist. The realization that theatre and spirituality, in the broadest sense, could be so intertwined utterly lit me up. I devoured everything I could find on Grotowski and became friends with the woman who wrote the first English-language biography of him. As soon as my university courses were complete, I received a grant to attend his legendary Theatre Laboratory in Wroclaw, Poland.

Grotowski soon became my first great mentor. At the height of his international acclaim, he had stopped his theatre work in order to more directly explore the further reaches of human consciousness. In Poland, as described earlier in this book, a small group of us were taken out to a forest, to a rundown stable block, which became our home for the next week.

We would be conducting an experiment, we were told: we were to cease all speaking, go together into the forest and surrounding countryside, and walk or run for hours on end. Although it was sub-zero February, we weren't allowed to wear coats or gloves. After returning, we could eat and then sleep for only two hours, after which we were awoken and directed back outside to start again. This routine went on for seven days. It was challenging, to say the least, but despite the intense cold and discomfort, we experienced moments of extraordinary connection, to each other and to the surrounding forest, meadows and streams.

The experience has been etched in me ever since. And it marked for me how essential the experience of embodiment is. For the next 20 years, I devoted myself to exploring and teaching heightened states of awareness with actors – in drama schools, including the prestigious Royal Academy of Dramatic Art in London, and later in my own company. The intense 'opening' experiences we achieved together were magical; there is almost nothing as beautiful or powerful as a human being whose every cell is alive with streaming energy and intelligence, as seen in truly great performances in music, dance or theatre. I devoted hundreds of hours of study to determining the practices that cultivate such openings, and how to induce these states intentionally rather than waiting for the occasional moment of grace to which every artist aspires.

On a never-ending quest, I trained in psychosynthesis, studied for two years with a Zen meditation master and for two years with a Hawaiian shaman, from whom I learned a very special kind of bodywork which I practiced professionally and later taught. Afterwards, I trained in the Pesso Boyden Psychomotor therapeutic system, which analyses the present-day effects of traumatic memories.

I read intensively, finding the works of Carl Jung and Ken Wilber particularly illuminating. I also pursued a passion for drumming, spending three months with the Kodo drummers in Japan and six months with a master-drummer in West Africa. I played concerts supporting Japanese master drummer Joji Hirota, and later created a percussion trio with whom I recorded two albums. Finally, I began leading intensive personal development workshops, retreats and year-long programmes. One of the highlights was co-leading with two colleagues a five-day retreat for 40 people in the Israeli desert. The retreat culminated in a 28-hour grief ritual, during which I drummed for 20 hours.

In 1997, I was part of the company that opened the reconstructed Globe Theatre in London with *Henry V*, directed by my close friend Richard Olivier. I composed and performed a percussion score for the production and supported Richard during the rehearsal process. We took the actors through processes from our respective personal development work, moving well beyond conventional rehearsal. It was an all-male company, echoing Shakespeare's time, and the group deeply bonded, delivering a production that was a fitting opening to such a special stage.

Around this time, Richard was invited to explore *Henry V* with a group of senior public sector managers. At the end of three days, the participants shared that they had learned more about leadership through the process than from any of the conventional management training programmes they had attended.

Hearing this lit a flame.

Already immersed in the Men's Movement of the time, Richard had an organization that hosted people like Robert Bly, Michael Meade and Malidoma Some for ritual retreats in the UK. To guide the group's process, retreat leaders often utilized characters and themes taken from historic myths and fairy tales. As we explored some of the greatest stories known to humankind, the penny dropped.

We found ourselves devoting more and more time to the development of a methodology we called Mythodrama, which used Shakespeare's stories as a developmental tool for senior leaders. We received great support from a visionary head of department at the Cranfield School of Management, and the work took shape. Though we each came from theatre careers, our capacity to understand and relate to the world of business leadership (a far region from any theatre!) evolved. Our running joke to participants: "We used to work with neurotic, insecure actors. Now, we work with neurotic, insecure executives." It always got just the right kind of nervous laugh.

Joined by master poet William Ayot, the work solidified and became more in demand. I never expected to leave the arts, but in 2001, Richard proposed to William and me that we quit theatre and create a consultancy. Thus, Olivier Mythodrama was born.

We were ahead of our time, rigorous about quality and our skill in the work continued to grow. This and the wisdom of Shakespeare brought us great success. We began travelling the world, delivering two to five-day retreats for senior leaders from all sectors, and trained new people to work with us.

For several years everything was wonderful, we were more successful than we could have imagined, yet some restlessness began to stir deep in my soul. These men were my dear friends, not just my colleagues, but I knew it was my time to go.

In the eight years since, I have poured my focus into developing the body of work that now culminates in *Leader as Healer.* I spent five years of study and practice under my most recent mentor, Thomas Hübl, a contemporary mystic in the truest sense of the word. Thomas has a remarkable capacity to work with peoples' very highest light *and* their deepest, most wounded parts. My training and friendship with him helped bring together all my previous years of study and practice.

After meeting and marrying my Israeli wife, and training in Thomas' powerful process designed to address collective trauma (often with large groups of Germans and Jews together), the depth of my father's suffering became clearer. And I recognized how the seeds of his trauma, however unacknowledged and unspoken, had been passed down to me – epigenetically, environmentally, culturally – and would, therefore, pass to my children unless I broke the chain. Leading ongoing groups devoted to personal, intergenerational and collective trauma healing in the UK, the US, Israel and the Middle East has given me a tremendous perspective on the degree to which our culture is affected far more than we realize by the hidden 'ghosts' of the past.

For many years, the primary subject of my work with leaders was on presence: what it means to show up with as much of oneself as possible. *Leader as Healer* is a natural deepening of the work, and I am moved and grateful for the way it has been received by leaders and organizations worldwide. Just a few years ago, this likely would not have been possible; after all, 'healer' isn't usually what we think of when we imagine CEOs and senior executives.

Leader as Healer is a response to the dangerous and growing fragmentation of our world, inner and outer. We have incredible technologies to aid us, but now we need equivalent development in consciousness. If we are to meet the systemic challenges and ecological crises of our time, if we are to enable our organizations to both thrive and contribute to society, our emotional, ethical and spiritual selves must also rise and grow. New and higher leadership capacities are possible and available, and are more urgently needed than ever. We have to learn to steward ourselves, our families, our organizations and our societies towards a healthier, more vibrant future for all.

I am wholeheartedly dedicated to serving the birth of those leadership capacities.

ENDNOTES

1. Otto Scharmer and Katrin Kaufer, *Leading from the Emerging Future*: (Berrett-Koehler, 2013)

2. Karyl McBride, PhD, "Understanding Narcissistic Injury," Psychology Today (October 25, 2020), accessed January 2021, https://tinyurl.com/y6925jsv

3. Jack McCullough, "The Psychopathic CEO," *Forbes* (December 9, 2019), accessed January 2021, https://tinyurl.com/y3zc2kwd

4. Iain McGilchrist, *The Master and His Emissary*: (Yale University Press, 2019)

5. Otto Scharmer and Katrin Kaufer, *Leading from the Emerging Future*: (Berrett-Koehler, 2013)

6. Subject-object theory was developed and advanced by American developmental psychologist Robert Kegan and can be explored further in his book, *The Evolving Self*: (Harvard University Press, 1982)

7. Bob Samples, *The Metaphoric Mind: A Celebration of Consciousness*: (Massachusetts: Adison-Wesley Publishing Company, 1976), p. 26

8. Alice G Walton, "7 Ways Meditation can Actually Change the Brain," *Forbes* (February 9, 2015), tinyurl.com/y4jf78lx

9. "What are brainwaves?" Brainworks Neurotherapy, accessed 13 December 2021, tinyurl.com/18o0kck1

10. Iain McGilchrist, "The Divided Brain," Ted Talk (RSA Animate, October 2011), https://www.ted.com/talks/iain_mcgilchrist_the_divided_brain

11. Iain McGilchrist, *The Master and His Emissary: The Divided Brain and the Making of the Western World*: (London: Yale University Press, 2012)

12. Miriam Greenspan, *Healing through the Dark Emotions: The Wisdom of Grief, Fear and Despair*: (Shambala, 2004)

13. David Whyte, *Consolations*: (Canongate Books, 2019)

14. Brene Brown, *Dare to Lead: Brave Work. Tough Conversations. Whole Hearts:* (Ebury Digital, 2018)

15. To learn more about the critical subject of collective trauma and what we can do to heal it, I recommend Julie Jordan Avritt and Thomas Hübl's 2020 book, *Healing Collective Trauma: A Process for Integrating Our Intergenerational and Cultural Wounds*

16. "Transgenerational inheritance of behavioural and metabolic effects of paternal exposure to traumatic stress in early postnatal life: evidence in the 4th generation," *Environmental Epigenetics*, Vol 4, Issue 2, (April 2018), https://doi.org/10.1093/eep/dvy023

17. Tori DeAngelis, "The legacy of trauma: An emerging line of research is exploring how historical and cultural traumas affect survivors' children for generations to come," *American Psychological Association*, Vol 50, No. 2 (February 2019); p.36

18. Ken Robinson and Lou Aronica, *Creative Schools: Revolutionizing Education from the Ground Up*: (Australia: Penguin UK, 2015)

19. Reginald Ray, *Touching Enlightenment: Finding Realization in the Body*: (Sounds True Inc, 2014)

20. Interview in *Rolling Stone* magazine May 2003

21. "Poor posture hurts your joints more than you realize: Three tips to fixing it," *Health Essentials*, (December 12, 2018), accessed February 2021, tinyurl.com/3ahdxkyp

22. Karina Kraska, "Poor Posture Affects More than Your Appearance," South Orange Chiropractic Center, (May 5, 2019), accessed February 2021, https://tinyurl.com/3htj7vfs

23. Keely Savoie, "7 Weird Ways Your Posture Messes with You," *Prevention*, (October 19, 2012), accessed February 2021, https://tinyurl.com/27h4sw7r

24. Joseph Campbell, *Power of Myth*: (Anchor, 1991)

25. "The Effects of Negative Ions," *Healthline,* (September 11, 2019), accessed February 2021, https://www.healthline.com/health/negative-ions

26. Afdhel Aziz, "The Power of Purpose: The Business Case for Purpose (All the Data You Were Looking for Pt 2)," *Forbes*, (March 7, 2020), accessed March 2021, https://tinyurl.com/kywn6maj

27. Annette Gann and Kelly Milburn, *Feel Good. Do Good. Work: How Caring is Great for Business*: (Independently published, August 28, 2020).

28. Studs Terkel, *Working*: (MJF Books, 2004)

29. Raj Sisodia and Michael J Gelb, *The Healing Organization: Awakening the Conscience of Business to Help Save the World*: (HarperCollins Leadership, 2021)

30. Nils Salzgeber, *The Happy Life Formula: How to Build Your Life Around the New Science of Happiness*: (Independently published, March 4, 2018)

31. In her book, *One Unknown*, author Gill Hicks tells the remarkable story of how losing both her legs in the 2005 London tube bombing transformed her life

32. Dee Hock, *Birth of the Chaordic Age*: (Berrett-Koehler, 1999)

33. Frances E Vaughan, *Awakening Intuition*: (New York: Anchor Books, 1979), p. 153

34. Interview *Rolling Stone Magazine* September 2014

35. Joseph Jaworski, *Synchronicity: The Inner Path of Leadership*: (San Francisco: Berrett-Koehler, 2011), p. 80

36. Erik Gregersen, "History of Technology Timeline," *Britannica*, (2021), https://tinyurl.com/5fh2danm

37. Otto Scharmer and Katrin Kaufer, *Leading from the Emerging Future: From Ego-System to Eco-System Economies*: (San Francisco, CA: Berrett-Koehler, 2013)

38. Michio Kaku, *Physics of the Future: How Science Will Shape Human Destiny and Our Daily Lives by the Year 2100*, (New York: Doubleday, 2011), p. 16

39. William F. Russell, *Second Wind: The Memoirs of an Opinionated Man*: (New York: Random House, 1979)

40. Jerzy Grotowski, *Towards a Poor Theatre*, ed., Eugenio Barba: (Oxfordshire, England: Routledge, 2002)

ABOUT THE AUTHOR

Over the last 20 years, Nicholas Janni has gained an international reputation for his transformational coaching and leadership development programmes, designed for chief executives, senior leaders and top teams from diverse sectors, public and private. His client list includes leaders at FedEx, Rolls Royce, Swiss Re, Teva Pharmaceutical Industries, Amdocs, Intel, Motorola, Microsoft, eBay and Lafarge, as well as the UK National Health Service, the UK Permanent Secretaries and several government ministers.

Originally a director of theatre, Janni taught acting at The Royal Academy of Dramatic Art in London and directed his own theatre company, The Performance Research Project. After dedicating 30 years of study to the theory and practice of 'the zone' – how to achieve flow states for peak performance – and to the study of multiple mind/body disciplines, Janni was led to work in the field of evolutionary leadership, consulting leaders and senior executives worldwide.

Today, his transformative work bridges the worlds of creative, personal, spiritual and professional development in a uniquely powerful, relevant and accessible way. Along with a one-to-one and group leadership consultancy practice, he leads programmes designed to address personal, intergenerational and collective trauma in the US, the UK and the Middle East.

In 1998, Janni became a Visiting Fellow at the Cranfield School of Management, UK, and in 2001 co-founded the arts-based leadership development consultancy, Olivier Mythodrama. Twelve years later, Janni founded his consultancy, Core Presence. He teaches at the prestigious University of Oxford Said Business School and at the IMD Business School in Lausanne.

Janni's work is devoted to helping leaders recognize and move beyond outdated mindsets, in order to meet the challenges of our time with far greater inner resources: to awaken to the fruits of simple contemplative and embodiment practices; develop mature awareness and integration of the emotions; and rebalance the capacities for reason, logic and analysis with those of empathy, awareness and intuition.

Michael Watkins, internationally bestselling author of *The First 90 Days*, has said: "I've asked Nicholas to teach in every major leadership development programme I run at the IMD Business School and elsewhere, because I've never seen anyone have a more sustainable, transformational impact on leaders than he does."

For more about Nicholas Janni and his work
in executive and leadership development
visit www.nicholasjanni.com

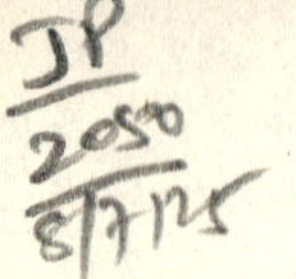